The
People of
God in
Ministry

The People of God in Ministry

William K. McElvaney

ABINGDON
Nashville

THE PEOPLE OF GOD IN MINISTRY

Library of Congress Cataloging in Publication Data
McELVANEY, WILLIAM K. 1928-
  The people of God in ministry.
  Includes bibliographical references.
  1. Pastoral theology. 2. Laity. 3. McElvaney, William K., 1928-
  I. Title.
BV4011.M25   253   80-26077

ISBN 0-687-30660-4 (pbk.)

MANUFACTURED BY THE PARTHENON PRESS AT
NASHVILLE, TENNESSEE, UNITED STATES OF AMERICA

To the memory of my parents, Sue and Eugene McElvaney,
who were my first and lasting ministers of Jesus Christ

Contents

Preface

The story of life is the story of one word. This book is about grace—God's love in action—that provides gifts and grit for Christian commitment.

Some books are written for the ordained clergy. Others are intended primarily for the laity. For a long time I've been convinced that few resources have been provided that bring clergy and laity together for mutual discovery, discernment, and discussion of Christian ministries. *The People of God in Ministry* is for this purpose.

The church's faithfulness to the gospel of Jesus Christ, and thus our effectiveness as an instrument of God's mission, depends on a difficult and delicate balance: commitment to a mutual ministry of one baptism, one faith, and one Lord, yet allowing for the utilization of the distinctive gifts and functions of the ordained and general ministries of the church. Having served as an adult layperson in three congregations prior to twenty-two years in the ordained ministry, I have reflected herein on the gifts and graces for an Easter People in a Good-Friday World . . . an Easter People made up of diverse clerical and lay ministries. In this journey I have not hesitated to draw on theology as autobiography, especially from fifteen years in the pastorate and seven years in theological education.

Clergy and laity can help each other through a growing awareness and appreciation for the faith formation of the other and the mutual responsibility in and for that development. While the first part of the book is a guide for the personal and professional development of clergy, it also provides an inside view for those laypersons who would look carefully and caringly into the shape of ordained ministry. Part II is a map assembled for lay study of the gifts and graces that God gives for the ministry of all Christians. My goal in those chapters is to assist the laity through a theologically oriented practical handbook in raising the pertinent questions of Christian commitment and imagining some directions for the future. For those clergy who are serious about the mutual ministry of all Christians, this latter section is intended to provide a beginning point for sharing the issues.

At the conclusion of each chapter, I have suggested questions for group discussion or personal reflection. *The People of God in Ministry* is intended to encourage your dreaming as well as your thinking and to call forth imagination and intuition as well as inquiry and insight.

I believe that inclusive language is basic to an emerging understanding of the Christian gospel and to a mutual ministry of all Christians. However, where using quotes that are not as inclusive as I would prefer, I have allowed the original language to stand in spite of my misgivings.

The late Thomas Hart Benton once said that many of his friends had given up their struggle to be alive to the challenges of the day, because they had become attached either to their comforts or to their miseries. My hope for these pages is that God's astonishing gifts (largess) to the Christian community will be exalted for the healing and hallowing of our mutual ministries through Jesus Christ. When this is our story, our attachments to life-deadening comforts and to life-defeating miseries are transformed into the growth pains, the consolation, and the joy that only God can give.

William K. McElvaney
February 1980

Acknowledgments

With each passing year I become increasingly aware of how much I owe to my former pastors, members of the congregations whom I've been privileged to serve, colleagues in the ordained ministry, and local churches and various conferences at which a considerable amount of this material has been presented in lectures and sermons. Trustee, faculty, staff, and student colleagues at Saint Paul School of Theology have contributed to my total efforts in this book. I am indebted in a special way to the Saint Paul School of Theology trustees for a one-month leave of absence for completion of the manuscript. Dr. William Sparks, Saint Paul School of Theology librarian, and the library staff have been immensely helpful in my research. Dr. Donald Treese, associate general secretary of the Division of Ordained Ministry, Board of Higher Education and Ministry, The United Methodist Church, provided valuable suggestions for chapters 1 and 2.

Jo Lafler, administrative assistant to the president at Saint Paul School of Theology, has become more proficient in reading my illegible handwriting than I. Her faithful transcribing into typewritten pages was indispensable for the project to get off the ground and to move toward completion. For her patience in retyping this or that section "one more time" I am extremely appreciative. The final manuscript was typed by Norma Damon, who likewise has aided me previously in a similar capacity. Once again, I am most grateful.

Part I

ORDAINED MINISTRY:

Impaled on the Horns of Joy

Chapter 1

THE ANATOMY OF ORDAINED MINISTRY

Section A

Ordained ministry is the most outlandish blend of beatitude and bedevilment yet invented by the mysterious and mischievous Divine Mind. No wonder there is an ancient bit of wisdom handed down through the centuries from those who know. Simply put, the counsel of the ecclesiastical sages concerning ordainment is this: "If you can do anything else, do it!"

If we placed a cross section of ordained ministry under a microscope, what would we see? What is the composition of responsibility and reward, weal and woe, agony and ecstasy?

In more than twenty years as an ordained minister I have seldom seen a *descriptive analysis* of the actual ingredients of our calling and profession. Much has been said and written about ministerial functions—the minister as preacher, teacher, priest, pastor, evangelist, planner, and so on with an almost endless assortment of variations. However, relatively little has been written to my knowledge which gets "inside" these functions, pointing to the characteristic day-by-day realities of ordained ministry.

In these first two chapters I propose to dissect the inner dynamics of ordained ministry in order to focus on the basic givens that are inherent in our work. Numerous persons and groups in the church have a stake in understanding and communicating these issues: pre-theological students, candidates for ministry, seminary students, committees on ordained ministry, supervising pastors, boards of ordained ministry, pastors and Pastor-Parish Relations Committees, seminary faculty, and seminary intern and field education departments.[1] Each denomination of course will have its own nomenclature for these interested parties.

The specifics of our anatomical focus will center on ordained ministry in the local church but will be more or less appropriate in other settings for ministry as well. My probing will include an autobiographical dimension arising from my own years in the ordained ministry of the local church and now as a seminary administrator, as well as observations from listening and interacting with colleagues in ordained ministry. The reader will need to provide the necessary variables according to settings for ministry and historical differences, including denominational, ethnic, and female experiences and viewpoints. In addition pastors of small churches and those in larger churches will translate into your circumstances. For forthcoming ordinands this material will provide a mechanism for gazing into your future. For those already ordained this material will challenge you to examine your ministry with a new pair of eyes and ears. These glimpses of burdens and blessings will not solve anyone's problems, but they can prompt you to introspection and intentionality about your ministry.

My purpose in these two initial chapters is to de-escalate the fantasy level that often attaches itself to ministerial calling and at the same time to strengthen the awareness of the unique joy that belongs to the very marrow of ordained ministry. To call the burdens and blessings of ministry by name is to discern more deeply their power either to erode or elevate our commitment. Since God made the world out of Crucifixion/Resurrection, the essence of ordained ministry is to be bound, burdened, and blessed by and for the ultimate promise and claim of God through Jesus Christ. The ministry is more than a patch of thorns, but it is not simply a rose garden. To be called to ordained ministry is to *be impaled on the horns of joy.*

The impalement and the joy belong to the same fabric of ministry. Thus in each case I have listed the identified characteristic as both burden and blessing. As the poet Blake expressed it, "Joy and woe are woven fine." The reader can decide where lies the weight of truth in your experience. The thirteen characteristics are by no means meant to be exhaustive, but they do provide in my opinion a fundamental framework for ordained ministry. It should be said that this descriptive analysis is not intended to be a biblical study per se of the nature of Christian ministry, although the connections with a biblical base will be apparent.[2]

Burdens and Blessings

1. The Absurdity of the Suffering-Sovereign Lord

Most of what I will be saying about burdens and blessings will have to do with the specific work of ordained ministry. However, ordained ministry needs to be seen first of all within an ever present more fundamental matrix: the gospel itself. The anatomy of ordained ministry always revolves around the pulsebeat of the gospel of Jesus Christ.

The *ambience* of the Divine-Human encounter is *ambivalence* on the part of humanity. We want the gospel. We resist the gospel. Jesus Christ is our rock, our hope, our deliverance. Jesus Christ is a threat to our demons, a head-on collision with our tendency to be either less or more than we were created to be (original sin as sloth or pride). Jesus Christ is always out of step with every age and with our individual lovelessness. Like the Gerasene demoniac (Mark 5), we move toward Jesus to worship and at the same time exclaim, "I adjure you by God, do not torment me," that is, do not disturb my demons! Paul Tillich, reflecting on Psalm 139, said that if we have never wished to escape from the living God of history, we must be worshiping a comfortable idol, a figment of our imagination. In ordained ministry we live with that all of our days.

As Paul insists in I Corinthians 1, the notion that a suffering, crucified, itinerant Jewish carpenter is the Sovereign Lord of history is an utter absurdity in terms of human wisdom. Indeed, is there a more astounding mystery than this: that the Suffering, Vulnerable One is also the Sovereign, Victorious One who is our source, our guide, and our reason for being?

In the grace of this One we are called to a life of sacrifice, stewardship, servanthood (not servitude or servility), and solidarity. As a response to Divine Love we are called to identify intentionally with the suffering of Christ and of humanity (Bonhoeffer's definition of a Christian in *Papers from Prison*). There is part of me, however, that wants to put considerable distance between myself and the hurts and sufferings of others; part of me that wants to be ensconced in comfort where nothing is going on; part of me that wants to reduce vulnerability and relentless responsibility; part of me that wants to say no to the ultimate yes.

Listen to a portion of John Wesley's Covenant Service that dates back to 1755:

> Christ has many services to be done; some are easy, others are difficult; some bring honor, others bring reproach; some are suitable to our natural inclinations, and temporal interests, others are contrary to both. In some we may please Christ and please ourselves; in others we cannot please Christ except by denying ourselves. Yet the power to do all these things is assuredly given us in Christ, who strengthens us.
>
> I am no longer my own, but thine. Put me to what thou wilt, rank me with whom thou wilt; put me to doing, put me to suffering; let me be employed for thee or laid aside for thee, exalted for thee or brought low for thee; let me be full, let me be empty; let me have all things, let me have nothing; I freely and heartily yield all things to thy pleasure and disposal.[3]

No pallid commitment this! In one manner of speaking a burden, in fact a crucifixion or death. Yet in a deeper sense the lightest imaginable yoke because from this death is born a whole spectrum of God's love: New Creation. Freedom. Wholeness. Reconciliation. Healing. Redemption. Salvation.

Liberation. The Suffering Lord of History is the Sovereign One!

Not only are we as ordained ministers personally involved with the death and rebirth of self vis-à-vis the gospel, but we also bear responsibility for this Word before the powers and principalities of the world. Jurgen Moltmann reminds us of both the strangeness and the power of the gospel in the world:

> In a culture that glorifies success and happiness and is blind to the suffering of others, remembering that at the center of the Christian faith there stands an unsuccessful, suffering, and shamefully dying Christ can open man's eyes to the truth, shatter the tyranny of pride and awaken solidarity with those who are hurt and humiliated by our culture.[4]

In the final analysis I suspect that it is the very absurdity or foolishness of the gospel that constitutes its redemptive power. This foolish quality of the gospel has drawn us into the community of Christ. It has attracted us and magnetized us. Ask any seminary student. It has wooed us and compelled us, even as it inevitably repels us by its demands. Ask any ordained minister worth New Testament salt. It has beckoned us and fascinated us with its first to be last and the last first. With its humble to be exalted and the exalted humbled. With its every mountain to be made low and every valley to be lifted up. This Impossible Possibility known as the gospel is our constant companion, our burden and blessing, our daily metabolism for all the days of our lives.

The absurdity of the Suffering-Sovereign Lord calls us to many *functions*, but to only one *focus*. Our single focus is the Word, Jesus Christ. We have too many functions to be classified as specialists in the classical or usual sense, yet in the covenant of the ordained we are specialists of the Word. In many roles and through diverse functions we have just this one purpose of lifting up and living out the Word. We are representatives of the Transcendent/Incarnational Lord. The ordained ministry of leading and empowering the people of God in and through God's Word in Jesus Christ is a task of proclamation, administering the sacraments, and representing the whole church *for which no one else in either church or society is trained.*

To be sure the total ministry of the Word is a mutual ministry of the whole people of God, visibly proclaimed in baptism and validated in the act of confirmation. An adequate theology of ministry can recognize the ordained as a specialist of the Word, and at the same time one who encourages a shared, collaborative style of leadership in and through the Word. As ordinands of the Word, we are in mutual pilgrimage with diaconal and general ministers of the church. The gospel itself calls us away from authoritarian leadership in favor of searching out and calling forth the total talents and gifts of the community of Christ.

The absurdity of the gospel of Jesus Christ calls us into an inevitable vortex of vulnerability and victory. The biblical witness and all theology derived from it knows no other theme. ". . . nothing happens outside of the paschal mystery. Our life is a continual reliving within ourselves of the paschal mystery—death and resurrection."[5] So our pastoral ministry is the paschal ministry of the Crucified/Risen One. Prepare for impalement on the horns of joy!

2. *Resonating with Constant Responsibility*

Ordained ministry is not a 9 to 5 job left at the church office by punching a time clock. There is no punch out! We take days off, we take vacations, and there are times we had best let the world turn without us. Woe to the congregation whose minister knows not how to play and relax. But the Suffering-Sovereign God does not take a vacation and neither does the suffering of the innocent nor the travail of the world. There is little or no control over the frequency and intensity of pastoral demands. In addition, ordained pastors are inextricably bound in varying ways with an organization made up of boards, councils, committees, and task forces. These groups involve a myriad of expectations, sometimes in strong conflict, to say nothing of institutional servicing involving budgets, maintenance, and administrative details. Even in the most highly developed mutual ministry where laypersons assume major responsibilities in these areas, there remains for the ordained minister a constant and demanding level of responsibility. Every potential ordinand should ask, "Do I want this much responsibility? Am I the kind of person who can wear well with these challenges?"

Of course you cannot answer this question experientially before you practice ministry for awhile. If you didn't believe that you were cut out for this work, you wouldn't be considering it in the first place. Besides, as Zorba the Greek exclaimed, "The Lord is a clever devil!" That means the Lord "blindsides" us just enough so that we don't fully know what we are doing, though we had better think we do. If we fully understood what we were getting into, we probably wouldn't have the courage to go through with any of the great decisions in life. If the Israelites had known the risks in the wilderness ahead of time, they never would have abandoned Pharaoh's fleshpots. The Lord shows us just enough to make us think we know what we're doing, yet it is Divine Grace upon which we depend.

The ongoingness of responsibility for ordained ministers in the local church is best highlighted by the weekly preaching task. Every seven days, whether you feel like it or not. Regardless of two funerals, a wedding, the need to study, a breakdown of your car, family budget problems, and what all else may occur in a given week. So at the appointed cosmic time on Sunday morning, you prepare not just to give a talk, but audaciously and humbly to speak *for God*. Every week we know the moment will come when we must take our stand. And every day of the week that moment comes closer, dangling there like the Sword of Damocles. How often I've wished that the Lord had made an eight-day week instead of seven in order to allow just one more day for sermon preparation! Or should I say for more procrastination?

I used to have this fantasy that preaching should be accorded the status of writing poetry. Whoever heard of a poet who had to produce on a ready-or-not treadmill? Let the preacher have adequate gestation time until the moment of rapture demands a proclamation to the people! No matter that this might take weeks or even months. My fantasy would call for ringing a giant bell (where this could be or how people would hear it is not clear) and a dramatic announcement that a divinely inspired word is about to come forth from the preacher's poetic and inspired tongue.

In *Joys and Sorrows* the great cellist Pablo Casals tells of an event which brought his first American tour to a sudden end. While climbing with friends on Mount Tamalpais in the San Francisco area, a loose boulder hurtled down the mountainside, smashing his fingering hand. "My friends were aghast. But when I looked at my mangled bloody fingers, I had a strangely different reaction. My first thought was, 'Thank God, I'll never have to play the cello again!' " I've yet to find a preacher who doesn't readily understand what Casals was saying. Casals goes on to say, "The fact is that dedication to one's art does involve a sort of enslavement, and then too, of course, I have always felt such dreadful anxiety before performances."[6]

I do not believe that anyone can serve for long in the ordained ministry without being aware of the regular responsibility involved. To prospective ordinands and to ministers in training, the church must raise the truthful question in love: "Do you think this much responsibility is for you?"

On the other hand—if we are convinced that we are called to preach, it is akin to what was known in the New Testament church as "apostolic compulsion." There is no other choice! To preach is to be, to become, a journey on the horns of joy from which there is no turning back. To preach is to actualize our own being in the Word, by the grace of that Word. For this we were born! "If I say, 'I will not mention him, or speak any more in his name,' there is in my heart as it were a burning fire shut up in my bones" (Jer. 20:9).

Those who bear the yoke of burden and blessing through preaching will need no interpretation of these audacious words of Martha Graham as we imaginatively apply them to preaching, as well as to our overall commitment to the Word:

> People have asked me why I chose to be a dancer. I did not choose to be a dancer. I was chosen to be a dancer, and with that you live all your life. When any young student asks me, "Do you think I should be a dancer?" I always say, "If you ask me that question, no! Only if there is only one way to make life vivid for yourself, and for others, should you embark upon such a career."[7]

The burden of high level responsibility and the corresponding level of high visibility that accompanies it is endemic to ordained ministry. It is, so to speak, the nature of the beast. Cornucopia is defined in Christian life in the form of kenosis, an emptying of oneself into life through the Word, a pouring out of life into life and for life. Responsibility as a response to grace and as always dependent on grace becomes the shape of our life journey. If there is no greater burden, neither is there any greater privilege or potential beatitude.

3. Vexations and Victories with Role Versatility

Closely related to the high level of responsibility is the simultaneous coordination of multiple roles required in ordained ministry, especially in local church ministry. As I have already suggested, the unifying thread that runs through all these functions is our specialty, the Word. This means that whether we are preparing a sermon, teaching a class, holding the hand of a cancer patient, training visitors, calling on an elderly person in need, having lunch with the lay leader, working with a community organization, planning the Sunday order of worship, or encouraging the hidden gifts of mutual ministers in the congregation, our overriding concern is the love of God in Jesus Christ and how that might come to life in the particular context of human lives.

In order to define the roles of ordained ministers, many authors have connected in various ways the ministry of Jesus and of the apostles to today's ministry. For example, James D. Smart sees continuity between Jesus and ministry today in the functions of preaching, teaching, and pastoring. These three are the forms of ministry in which the nature of Jesus' ministry found expression. "In all three (forms), Jesus is the shepherd seeking the lost, the herald of the Kingdom, the servant of all."[8]

The complexity of ministry in today's world has brought forth a proliferation of duties for the ordained ministry, a fact that needs careful evaluation. However, even with meticulous scrutiny and with movement toward the mutual ministry of laity and clergy, there are few work descriptions that require a wider array of talents and skills than the ordained ministry of the local church. One has only to read an average day in almost any pastor's log or journal, if such were recorded, to realize the truth in this assertion. These many roles inevitably expose us to a wide range of conflicting expectations, including our own internalized ones as well as those from spouse (if married), denominational leaders, clergy peers, community sources, and members of the congregation.

The attempt to coordinate the wide latitude of role versatility is at times like an ecclesiastical juggling act. There are bound to be frustrations of too many competing claims and insufficient time to provide in-depth responses. Sometimes we have to accept this as one of our burdens. At the same time these "givens" of ordained ministry offer an almost unrivaled opportunity for personal maturation. Whatever else ordained ministry may be, it is for sure a "growth" calling and profession. Stagnation can of course occur, but I believe you have to work at it for that to happen!

Ministry with its role versatility is by nature a *self-reflective* vocation, yet at the same time a *relational* vocation. How can we prepare sermons or participate in pastoral caring without looking both inward and outward, without experiencing new discoveries of God, self, and world? How can we teach others without learning and growing? How can we minister to children and not be better off for it? And how can we be concerned with and involved in the great issues of our historical era apart from a process of maturation?

Most people in our society are engaged in product and profit oriented work. Ministers are given to people-oriented activities through the covenant community called into being by the Christian gospel. The Protestant insistence, built upon New Testament teaching, has always been—at least in theory—that God's world is one world and that God is active and present in all spheres and dimensions, in powers and principalities as well as prayer and piety. Although the ordained ministry is no more holy or "religious" than other forms of work according to the Protestant principle, I do believe it offers in its bewildering assortment of roles and functions an unusual invitation to growth-in-depth as a human being.

One of the factors that makes theological education a particularly demanding experience is that both professors and students are so very much themselves an inevitable part of the subject matter. While any profession is concerned with personhood as well as professional content and method, this is doubly so of ordained ministry. Students of economics or law can concentrate on the content of subject matter without major reference of personal identity and relationship to the content studied. Theological study involves the whole person, touching the multidimensional range of the intellectual, spiritual, and functional. The framework of theological study encompasses the student's own human condition as a sinner, as a recipient of God's grace, and as one immersed in the ultimate issues of life and death. In his book, *The Integrity of Worship,* Paul Waitman Hoon mentions a seminarian who once suggested that "to enter

25

the ministry is to choose the vocation one would most like to be a sinner in."[9] Precisely.

Thus, ordained ministry offers the challenge of demanding yet broadening intellectual, functional, and interpersonal requirements combined with spiritual discipline. No other work calls for so much, yet offers so much. What other daily commitment asks for the discipline and the freedom of spiritual growth? What other calling beckons us to such a variety of persons and situations in so many different roles? Where else are we mandated to contemplation, scholarship, and community involvement? Who among us could even imagine a work that may combine the mundaneness of mimeographing with the mystery of sacraments? And what other work calls for such a spectrum of knowledge—theology, psychology, sociology, history, the arts?

In Wesley's "An Address to the Clergy" in 1756, he spoke of a well-furnished minister. The "furnishings" included some knowledge of the sciences, logic, metaphysics, natural philosophy, geometry, profane history, ancient customs, and geography. Today we would add the importance of new knowledge from social sciences and fields of human behavior. This is to say that ordained ministry is concerned about *all of life* and thereby is inevitably a complex calling and endeavor.

In reflecting on role versatility and the time bind that ordained ministers so often experience, the role of student—scholar–theologian is extremely prominent. Ordained ministry is a "book" profession that demands constant reading and reflection. The Bible is our "book of books," our constant touchstone for all the far corners of ordained ministry. John Burkhart puts it like this: "A sure index of whether a seminary is doing its proper job well is the way and skill with which its graduates use the Bible throughout the years of their ministries, since actually no degree of theological sophistication or measure of practical know-how can finally compensate for deficiencies in biblical understanding."[10]

It is no accident that the work space of most professionals is called an office whereas an ordained minister's space is referred to as a study (even if it isn't). Since ordained ministry is irrevocably linked with the Bible and with a historical tradition, our ministry is related to the past in a unique manner among the professions. If you tire easily of reading, research, and mind-stretching, you won't last long in the ordained ministry of the local church. Or at least you shouldn't! In recollecting his fascinations with ministers while yet a youth in his hometown, Harvey Cox relates, "They had huge collections of books, were actually *paid* to read them. . . ."[11] It goes with the calling!

Role versatility and all that comes with it can be very frustrating, but it can also be a very freeing path toward wholeness and the hallowing of life.

4. *The Bittersweet Yoke of Freedom*

Although ordained ministry is consumed with countless diverse tasks and with many relational encounters or transactions, there is a high level of freedom. As a pastor you are pretty much your own daily supervisor. In spite of the fact that your agenda is partially determined by other people and by regularly calendared events, a great deal of self-direction, intentionality, and time management skills are necessary for competent fulfillment of ordained ministry.

One of the most frequent problems mentioned by most pastors is the need for creative use and management of time. This need arises from the already mentioned high level of responsibility and wide range of role versatility, mixed with the freedom of choice that comes from being your own manager. I can think of many kinds of work in which there is less complexity, less uncertainty of schedule, and less freedom to decide so many things so regularly. If you like decision-making, you'll love the ordained ministry!

The presence of freedom and the constant need for decisions

point to a fact about ordained ministry that is too seldom recognized: much of ordained ministry is performed *alone,* especially where there is no multiple or parish staff for the sharing of ordained functions. Of course possessive and controlling styles of ministry accentuate aloneness, since others are denied their own creative gift-giving for a mutual ministry between clergy and laity. But even in a genuine mutual ministry style, there remains a considerable amount of work done alone by the pastor.

Except for group study and continuing education with other clergy and laypersons, the pastor's study time is frequently done alone. Most time in personal spiritual discipline and devotion is time alone. Sermon preparation is usually a solo process. Where laypersons or other clergy share in the effort, it is more likely to be the exception than the rule. When a pastor makes hospital or home calls, the time spent in coming and going is alone time. A certain amount of administrative work, even in a truly collegial style, is bound to be done alone.

Ordinands need to be aware of this characteristic of ordained ministry. An individual who cannot work effectively in the latitude of freedom and individual decision-making of ordained ministry will find it extremely difficult. The majority of ordained ministers have their office in a building where there is no other staff, or no more than a secretary. Thus, working alone is a given. In many other kinds of work people function in clusters of offices involving a number of other persons. Furthermore, the vast majority of laypersons are involved in their own places of work during regular daytime office hours, either in or beyond the home. Thus, they are simply not available when the pastor is doing much of her or his own work.

If a high level of freedom with its inherent requirement for time management can be a burden, it is of course also an opportunity to be treasured. If some degree of working alone is difficult, it can also be a source of personal renewal translated into more effective ministry for others. Freedom has never been easy to handle, as the Exodus story with its subsequent experience in the wilderness so well reminds us. We prefer predictable routine and grooved channels that reduce the anxiousness of responsible freedom. Yet it is through the imaginative and disciplined use of freedom that our own personhood develops and out of which emerges an intentional ministry.

Effective time management can be enhanced in many ways. Some pastors regularly imagine an agenda for the next day, with plans and priorities ready but necessarily flexible to receive the unexpected changes that in a general sense can be expected. Other pastors have learned how to record their use of time over a stipulated period in order to analyze where the time goes and what that says about themselves and the demands of their work. An *awareness* of the use of time and the fact of time spent alone can enable freedom of decision and self-direction to become one of the remarkable challenges of our ministry.

5. *For Better or Worse: Covenant Community/Institutional System*

Ordained ministry is irrevocably linked, for better or for worse, with a community of people and an institutional system. The obviousness of this fact should not overshadow the momentous meaning behind it. Some of the most agonizing vexations of ordained ministry arise from this connection, as do some of the most victorious and enjoyable experiences of life. In my ministry I have found that the apparent disadvantages of this relationship have had corresponding or offsetting advantages. The particulars of course will vary according to denominational polity and practice, and with individual experience and interpretation of that experience.

I have a close friend who is a psychiatric social worker. For contrast I have often reflected on his situation as compared to ordained ministry, especially as I have known it in The United Methodist Church. Basically he is a counselor who works with his own clients, some of whom are referred by either ministers

29

or psychiatrists. He has his own office and sets his own hours. He is assured of the continuing residence of his choice, since he is not related to an itinerant ᵉystem to which he has given control over his future job assignments, as well as over his spouse's choice of work opportunities and the location of his children's educational experience through the twelfth grade. He has no reports to make and free weekends if he so chooses with the occasional exception of a client's emergency call. He does not have to contend with the possibility of contentious or narrow-minded persons from whom he draws his salary and who may evaluate him with his superior. He has no worries with living in houses that are not the choice of his own family and has a minimum of property or housekeeping details related to his occupation. Finally, he has a virtual immunity from decisions emanating from "higher" places, such as cabinets or national conferences.

Of course this example does not represent the working situation of most people, but I mention it to be a constructive provocateur. One could just as easily use examples that would typify the situation of the vast majority of our society, situations that by most standards would seem to be much less desirable.

One of the most frequent complaints voiced by local church pastors is the "Gestetner Gestalt" meaning the endless amount of housekeeping chores and details consuming energy and time. Could it be that underneath our expression of woe there is part of us that desires to retain these chores? Mailing the newsletter or setting up a room for a meeting are, relatively speaking, measurable and tangible with a smaller contamination of ambiguity compared with pastoral care and preaching. Or could it be that we need to clarify with our Pastor-Parish Relations Committee or its equivalent the role of the clergy and that of laity? Or might it be that our professional status has placed us "above" such mundane chores? Although it hasn't always brought solace to my protesting instincts, I believe it doesn't hurt to remind ourselves that the Body of Christ needs a certain amount of nose wiping and diaper changing as well as lofty goals and ideals. Neither does it hurt to remember that the majority of the world's people are constantly involved in the mundane care of people and institutions, that is, if they have work at all.

Regardless of what examples may be used in other kinds of work, either seemingly advantageous or disadvantageous in comparison with ordained ministry, the burdens of being connected with a covenant community/institutional system should not be disguised or denied. Any and all methods of ministerial placement have their undesirable features, fraught with human frailties and foibles.

Sometimes we are called upon to make the best of an unwanted situation. And often times God moves beyond our pride and our obstinance. In 1958, I completed nine months of special graduate theological studies at Union Theological Seminary in New York. Returning to Texas, I was led to believe that I would receive an appointment to begin a new church in a sizable city. At almost the last minute, the appointment was changed to a rural community of which I'd never heard. After struggling with anger, self-pity, and secretly threatening to become a Presbyterian, I went to my new rural setting because that was my appointment. At 5 A.M. on the very first morning, fresh from thirty years of urban life, I learned the meaning of ontological shock when that rooster crowed just outside my window. It was a long way from New York City! The parsonage doorknobs were loose and a company of mice inhabited the premises. To make matters worse I knew nothing about farming and rural life. During that year the parishioners taught me a lot about ministry and about warm caring love.

I wasn't much in the kitchen and soon I was dining with members in their homes or at the Dairy Queen on the highway operated by a blind member of our congregation. I've often chuckled that perhaps my main gift to the local church during that year was that I literally starved the mice out of the parsonage. This first twelve-month assignment has remained in my affections through the years although I did not originally want to be there. If God can bring resurrection out of crucifixion, surely those of us who do ministry in the Easter Name can turn some personal disappointments into meaningful experiences. Many years later I learned the reason for the last-minute appointment change. The handful of people who had talked with the bishop about a new suburban church in their area did not want an unmarried pastor!

An institutional system can confront us with many questionable practices baptized by time, custom, and familiarity. Some of these are very slow to change. For example the roles expected of clergy spouses and families by church members can sometimes be extremely frustrating. Systems of remuneration often defy explanation, especially on a theological basis. There is no denying that opting into a community of people and an institutional system is a decision to accept certain limits and restrictions.

However, this same set of circumstances offers a ready-made base for multiple ministries with all kinds of people. No other setting provides an ongoing opportunity for preaching to covenant colleagues with whom we participate in pastoral care and mission in the wider community. Can we imagine a situation that immediately opens as many doors literally and figuratively into individual lives as well as community life? The accessibility and potential of human and material resources for ministry is a given in almost every setting for ordained ministry.

Probably no one would claim that ordained ministry is a likely path to a lucrative lifetime income by secular measurements. If that's your goal, you're in the wrong place. Even so, there is usually a ministry available in most denominations for ordained ministers in good standing. While pastors formerly were considerably more nomadic than our society in general, this is probably no longer the case considering the accelerated mobility of the American people. At least when the ordained minister moves, especially if she or he is ministering in a local congregation, there are almost sure to be caring persons waiting and looking for you on the other end of the move. Without any question I regard the friendship of so many persons with whom I have ministered in several congregations to be one of the richest blessings of my life. Every institutional system will have its drawbacks, but every Christian community will have its gifts and graces.

6. The Ambience of Ambiguity

The "bottom line" in ordained ministry is not as measurable as in some types of work. Profits can be measured. So can sales and expenses. *Meaning* in people's lives is frequently more difficult to assess. Love is not easily quantified, nor is truth in complex situations. A sacramental perception of human existence that depends on divine grace is not easily calibrated. Neither are the mysteries of God for which we are stewards and interpreters. Value education or clarification knows no simple verification.

As one minister exclaimed, "There are a lot of 'ungetatibles' in our work." In spite of the sense of well-being when all the pews are filled or our membership records indicate an upswing, we know— unless we hide it from ourselves—that these visible signs are not automatically guarantees of the truth and liveliness of the gospel. The societal assurances of success are frequently absent or considerably truncated in ordained ministry, such as measurable so-called usefulness and visible acquisitiveness of things. Woody Allen has remarked how nice it would be if God would demonstrate the certainty of divine existence: "If only God would give me some clear sign! Like making a large deposit in my name in a Swiss bank."

Yet the very characteristic of ambiguity in ordained ministry may save us from self-justification or dependence on false supports. In a previous book I put it this way: "blessed are we

33

when we can affirm life in the midst of its ambiguities and ambivalences since this is the only kind of life there is. And God's Grace offers us precisely the freedom to do so. This has to be either the best news we've ever heard or else an ultimate threat to our compulsions to be absolutely right, to be absolutely certain, and to be absolutely in control. No wonder Jesus was crucified by some while others claimed he was the Messiah."[12]

In ordained ministry—as for life itself Christianly understood—the journey in Jesus Christ is its own intrinsic meaning and significance. The explorer Wilfred Grenfell said that "genuine joy grows not from riches or fame, but from work that has its own inner value." Pablo Casals claimed that "one's work should be a salute to life."[13] The late Thomas Hart Benton holds before us the view (read it by substituting the word minister or ministry for the word art or artist): "The rewards of art for the artist are concomitants of its practice. They lie in the life-heightening acuteness of everyday occupational experiences."[14]

Of course I can think of some days when "occupational experience" feels like a disaster, days when the practice of ministry seems like a life-deadening experience. But if we are right for ordained ministry and if it is right for us, the journey over a period of time will indeed be one of rich reward and gratification. In a television program about the life of Pope John XXIII when he was Cardinal Roncalli, several scenes told of his attempts to identify with the helpless and the outcasts of society. At one point he was concerned especially for the saving of the lives of a group of Jewish children from the Nazi terror. In one scene his sister scolds him, inquiring as to what his ministry has amounted to over the years with its repeated concern for the "nobodies" of society. His reply was simply, "The reward for the past forty years is the past forty years." Amidst all the ambiguity there is a special joy and glory.

I have come to believe that in ordained ministry the frustration, the hurts, and the anguish are perhaps greater than in any other work. But I also believe that joy and beatitude are more profound. When all is said and done there are plenty of us who believe—fools that we are—that ministry with all of its ambiguity, is a calling and work of ultimate certitude. Heaven and earth will pass away and only the Word remains. Our specialty is the Word, Jesus Christ—a Word for all seasons and for all time.

For Reflection and Discussion

1. Where is your weight of experience as you balance these burdens and blessings of ordained ministry?
2. In what area do you most need help for hurting, and what new possibilities can you imagine?
3. What burden/blessing in particular would be fruitful for discussion with either your lay leaders or ecclesiastical leaders?
4. Suggested exercise for pastors: Invite your Pastor-Parish Relations Committee (or its equivalent) to read this chapter, as well as chapter 2, in preparation for discussion and mutual understanding.

Chapter 2

THE ANATOMY OF ORDAINED MINISTRY

Section B

The tension of burden and blessing in ordained ministry carries a unique message about our calling and profession. The message is this: The ordained ministry is not for everyone, and to be in it if it is not right for you is a bedeviled form of agony without ecstasy. However, the opposite is just as true. To be right for ordained ministry—to experience the sense of urgent call and "meant-to-be" inner imperative—and *not* to be in it can also be a peculiar form of unsettling anguish. While a sense of call is no guarantee that ordained ministry is meant to be your lifetime destiny, there can be a relentless sense of being haunted and hounded by the question of ordained ministry until the dilemma is settled.

With these matters in mind, we are ready to probe further into the anatomical burdens and blessings of ordained ministry.

1. Clergy and Laity Differentials

Theologically speaking we know that clergy and laity alike compose the laos, the people of God. We know that we have a common ministry in Jesus Christ through the sacrament of baptism. Our mutual ministry through covenant with God and one another calls us all, whether general, diaconal, or ordained ministers, to a life of outreaching love in response to Jesus Christ. In the ministry of Christians there is no part-time covenant.

When we shift gears and speak in the language of practical experience, however, it is important for the ordained minister to make his or her peace with an inevitable *differential* in the covenant community. Not that it necessarily should be this way but that to some extent it always *is* this way. And the sooner we can accept it, the sooner we can cease a fruitless anger with all of its frustrations and begin to cope creatively with the reality at hand.

I'm speaking of the fact that most of the time the ordained will be more convinced of the priority of the church in relation to everything else than will a good percentage of church members. This is not a jaundiced or pejorative view of the general ministers of the church. The ordained minister believes that the church in its many forms, whether gathered or dispersed as mission to the world, is an urgent matter. Otherwise a life commitment to the ordained ministry would be a self-contradiction (keeping in mind that the form of ministry may vary greatly). Even with appropriate theological and psychological "distance" from the church, so that the church becomes neither an idol in the place of God, nor a surrogate identity for the pastor, it is still the case that the ordained will "live and breathe" the life of the church.

Ordained clergy need to remember that many of our church members spend their daily lives in extremely difficult work and home situations occupying an enormous amount of their physical and emotional energy. Thus, some functions of the church, such as committee meetings and planning sessions, may not seem as urgent to the laity at times as they may to us. Again, this is not to say that church members are less committed to *the gospel* in the totality of their life, nor less committed to the *purpose* of the Christian church. Some may in fact be *more* committed. But as far as availability for different kinds of gatherings and meetings is concerned, clergy are full-timers and laity are part-timers.

While we can speak of equal responsibilities in many ways, the ordained do have particular accountability in other ways; for example, preaching the Word from week to week. In theory both the clergy and laity are committed to be the worshiping

Body of Christ. In practice the clergy cannot stay at home on Sunday morning except for illness or similar reasons. We don't stay at home because company dropped in, and we don't run down to the lake. In both the category of *time* and that of *function,* of Word, order and sacrament, there is a bound-to-be differential to be recognized and accepted.

The acceptance of this time and functional differential can do several things for the clergy. It can ward off self-pity and at the same time keep us from laying guilt trips on the laity when they do not meet our expectations. More importantly this acceptance can lead us to appreciate the faithfulness of so many laypersons and to underscore our mutual ministry in Jesus Christ. The clergy's task includes that of drawing forth the gifts of God already present in God's people. In the process the clergy will also be enabled and enlightened. If we see laypersons as means to ministerial ends, as helpers to fulfill our need to control, then there will likely be a sense of disappointment and discouragement. If we see laypersons as colleagues in shared ministry, there is more likely to be growth and excitement for all.

Two other clergy-laity differentials are equally important. It has sometimes been said that the role of the clergy is primarily to serve the church whereas the task of the laity is basically to serve the world. A partial truth is contained in this viewpoint but it needs to be more precisely stated. Jesus Christ died for the world, not for the church. Thus the church exists for the world. Because this is so, the role of the entire church—clergy and laity—is none other than to serve the world. Putting it this way insists that all Christian ministry is a means to the end of mission in the world. The ecclesiastical differential can now appropriately be articulated: clergy serve the world primarily through the church's ministry of Word, sacrament, and order. The laity serve the world primarily through the church's ministry of multidimensional presence in the arenas of public life. More than one writer has commented that the clergy is the church *sacral* in the world and the laity is the church *visible* in the world.

The distinction is significant. If busy church work replaces the work of the church in the world, the ministry of the laity becomes a self-centered incarceration of the Good News. If clergy see the church as an end in itself, our ministry will become enslaved to an institutional idol. On the other hand if we as clergy forget that our role in serving the world is primarily through Word, sacrament, and order, we may usurp the role of the laity and fail in the difficult task of helping prepare them for their primary ministry in the world. While I believe that the clergy should be involved in the public arenas of life, this participation should not be a substitute for the sometimes more difficult task of preparing the laity for the mission of the whole church in the world.

A third clergy-laity differential is lifted up by Richard John Neuhaus when he speaks of "The Burden of Holiness": "I do believe that those who aspire to the (ordained) ministry must be prepared to bear the burden of holiness. . . . They are an order set apart . . . to bear public witness to another world of which this world is part."[1] Harvey Cox points in the same direction in his reminiscence of the ministers who came and went during his childhood:

> They were never completely at home in Malvern. . . . the minister always came from somewhere else, stayed a few years, then left. . . . The preacher, even if he stayed five years, was always to some extent a stranger in a strange land. Maybe that gave him a little of the aura of transcendence or at least of the "otherness" the representative of God must always signify, whether he likes it or not.[2]

The validity of this differential will be affirmed by some, either as the way things are or as the way it should be. Others will object on the basis that mutual ministry is thereby discouraged. Are not all Christians called to holiness or to the obedient life in Christ? And is there not already a false expectation, either by some ordained ministers and/or by some of the laity, that a clergyperson should be someone super human or super holy and thus actually less than human?

Theologically the church struggles with the tension between an expectation of exemplary leadership from those who have taken ordination vows and an insistence on one Lord, one baptism, and one faith. To be sure both laity and clergy are accountable to the Lord of history for the claim of the gospel on their lives. Yet from an ecclesiastical viewpoint ethical behavior for a layperson is likely to be regarded as a *personal* matter whereas clergy ethical behavior is more likely to be seen as a *professional* issue related to accountability to an office or function of the church. Perhaps the matter is put into perspective in these words: "In no other profession are the philosophy and performance of the vocation so intimately entwined with the commitments, values, and behavior of one's private life, in the eyes of those who serve and those who are served."[3]

If as ordained ministers we seek a ministry in which personal example is not intimately related to our practice of ministry, the differential of which I've been speaking can only be a burden to us. But if we see our personal example as part of the fabric of our ministry that God can utilize, then we will learn the blessing of our dependence on the grace of God.

2. The Combination of the Personal and the Social

As much as I appreciate the opportunity to be a counselor, and in spite of some of the great experiences of my life in this capacity, I'm not sure that I'd want to be a full-time counselor. Nor would I want to work eight hours every day of the week for fair housing, although some of my most cherished memories in pastoral ministry are related to involvement in this issue.

The diversity and the interrelatedness of our role versatility constitute part of the excitement of ordained ministry in the local church. Like the biblical heritage itself, our ministry is a combination of the deeply personal and the profoundly social. Among those who have served in the local church as ordained ministers, who would not value the occasions of pastoral caring and the privileges of sharing both the joys and sorrows of another's life? And who among us would not give thanks for those times when the ministry has called us to work for improvement of a social ill or when we could do no other than to identify with the powerless against unjust powers and principalities? What other work offers this remarkable and demanding combination?

If you want to work full-time on social problems in a direct sense, the ministry of the local pastorate is not for you. The bulk of our time is spent with the needs of individuals. This is not to diminish the responsibility for social caring and witness. It is simply to recognize the reality of ministry in the local church. I used to be amused that my ministry in the local church was sometimes identified by critics as majoring too much in social concerns, such as fair housing, protest against the Vietnam War, concern for hungry people and for justice in the school system. While some of these efforts occasionally were reported in the media, what was not reported was the 90 percent of my time spent from day to day in preparing sermons, making hospital calls, working with church school teachers, writing newsletters, catching up on correspondence, and calling on prospective members.

On the other hand if you do not want in some way to relate the gospel to the great issues of our time, I would strongly urge staying away from the ordained ministry. Liberation theologies are pointing to the immensity of human suffering in our world, and to the church's calling to preach good news to the poor, and to set at liberty those who are oppressed. An ordained pastor whose parish is only the parish presently being served, rather than the world as Wesley put it, needs to take a new look at what it means to represent Jesus Christ and to fulfill faithfully the representative character of the ordained ministry. "The ordained ministry is defined by its intentionally representative character, by its passion for the hallowing of life, and by its concern to link all local ministries with the widest boundaries of the Christian community" (*The Book of Discipline of the United Methodist Church* 1980, Paragraph 109).

An unusually perceptive treatment of the pastor's prophetic function was woven together by Harold A. Bosley in a paper entitled, "The Minister as a Creative Critic." He regards the ordained ministry "as the creative edge of the church" and the role of creative critic "as a central vocation of their ministry. It is our calling to articulate a religious tradition which has steadily maintained that, in God's sight, nations, however powerful they may be when viewed in the perspective of military and material means, are in reality helpless if they set themselves against [God's] holy will." He goes on to say, "The task of bringing the life of our day under the judgment of God is one of the most ancient and honorable ones in our tradition. . . . [The prophets] laid claim to the whole domain of life for God's sake. They criticized morals, politics, foreign policy, and religious institutions. . . . They made many mistakes, to be sure, in their efforts; but they never made the worst mistake of all, that is, of believing and acting as though some part of life were separable from the claim of God as we see it in Jesus Christ."[4]

The ordained ministry is forever under the Lordship of one who is out-of-step with the way things are in our world. The burden of creative critic in Christ's name should not be underestimated, even when exercised faithfully, strategically, and intelligently. But there are few moments in life greater than when we have held forth the Word without favor, knowing that we must obey God rather than powers or principalities. To speak the truth (as we understand it) in love is an unsurpassed privilege and responsibility of ordained ministry, a sacred trust requiring faithful homework and sensitivity to people as well as to issues.

Individual and social caring are extensions of each other. Together they constitute the difficult joy that is so unique in ordained ministry.

3. The Comprehensiveness of Ordained Ministry in the Local Church

We often take for granted those matters that have come to seem obvious because they are simply part of the landscape. Since certain givens are part and parcel of ministry in the local church, we tend to forget—or perhaps never even initially realize—the genuinely amazing gifts that are there before we ever arrive on the scene. I'm thinking of the fact that through the local church ministry an ordained minister is in a position to serve *every* person regardless of race, class, age, sex, and nationality. Furthermore, the pastor is frequently in a position to serve the whole person more than anyone else. When you think about it, this is an astounding combination of possibilities.

Our "union card" will ordinarily be a door opener into people's homes, their business, and into various community organizations. An ordained minister has access to people in the community beyond the church membership, as well as through various ministries of the local congregation. The same possibility holds true in regard to a liberating ministry with people of different races. The theological foundations of the church and of ministry call forth an outreaching love to all persons.

Since the biblical witness is one that relates to the whole person—spiritual, religious, intellectual, physical, social—our ministry is concerned for *wholeness* for the whole person. Biblical theology is content neither to save souls apart from human conditions nor to become an uncritical ideology for programmatic social change. The gospel holds before us a total relationship to God and a total ministry of wholeness. Wholeness of life. Wholeness of society. Wholeness of spirit and wholeness of structure. Wholeness of prayer and wholeness of politics. In this sense ministry is comprehensive by its very nature.

Another component of this comprehensiveness has to do with family and with age. The synagogue and the church are among the few social structures in our society that are related to all members of the family regardless of age. Few institutions and few professions have the many-sided transactions with persons of different age and with the intergenerational dimensions represented in families as do the church and the pastor. In the light of so much personal, family, and social disintegration, the enormous possibilities provided through the Christian congregation and the ordained ministry in the intergenerational sphere is no less than astounding. If you're looking for a challenge, here's one that will consume a lifetime and then some.

The comprehensive and holistic nature of ordained ministry can be experienced as a burden because it increases our need for a many-sided knowledge in the face of complexity, taxes our capacity for discernment to the limit, and reduces our areas of self-protection that would be available in a less challenging role. The blessing is in the magnitude of the possibilities for ministry.

4. Inevitable and Frequent Evaluation

The ordained minister is frequently scrutinized, sized up, and evaluated, if not officially then informally and unofficially. As a result an ordained minister is called upon to receive both praise and criticism. Either can destroy. Either can build up.

Evaluation's inevitability is occasioned partly by the fact of leadership itself. Anyone in the position of a leader, even in a shared style, is "a lightning rod" who will draw criticism for diverse reasons. Since the ordained ministry represents an ultimate authority to many people, and because it is both public and personal, it is especially vulnerable to illogical responses.

For many clergy persons the sermon is the most sacrosanct

area of evaluation. I've heard many church leaders, both lay and clerical, exclaim that a certain minister could receive criticism on just about any ministerial function except preaching. A deeply felt appreciation for the sermon brings a special gratification to the preacher. A negative response, either by those present or by virtue of sustained absence, is especially difficult to accept. Yet this function is bound to be near the top of the laity's list for evaluation.

Martin Luther had an extremely valuable word at this point for future generations of clergy as well as for his own. "The ministers of the Gospel should be men who are not too easily affected by praise or criticism, but simply speak out the benefit and the glory of Christ and seek the salvation of souls." He goes on to say, "To preach the Gospel for praise is bad business, especially when people stop praising you. Find your praise in the testimony of a good conscience."[5]

If evaluation is too harsh, or if our capacity to receive reasonable and constructive criticism is too limited, it can become a heavy burden. Evaluation can also represent a growth factor in ministry that strengthens the ordained minister as a person and as a professional. Much depends on skills and openness in giving and receiving evaluation. One of the most significant trends in the life of the church today is the increasing attention given in seminaries and in church structures on feedback, measurements, and evaluation. Chapter 5 will include further reflections thereon.

Through the years I've seen praise and appreciation virtually save a person's ministry. But I've also seen clergy persons allow themselves to be seduced by flattery and praise. Most of us have experienced painful growth through various kinds of evaluation, both sought and unsought. When I look back over my years in the ordained ministry, I realize that with time and emotional distance I can affirm the importance of those persons who came across as crotchety critics. Perhaps I learned more about myself—my need to control, to be liked and be praised, to be comfortable—from the irascible than from the irenic. We can count on the grace of God to give us both, and we need both.

Everything depends totally on the grace of God. But in the context of that grace, whether or not a given circumstance is more blessing or burden depends totally on us.

5. A Ministry Sent: Good-bye to the Sedentary

Whereas psychologists and other counselors expect clients to take the initiative in coming for services to be rendered, ordained ministry is a "sent" calling and profession. The essence of Christian ministry is moving toward people and taking the initiative for availability. This availability is not limited to any special group or requirement, such as financial ability or status in the community.

The itinerate style of United Methodist clergy is not to be restricted to appointments and "moves." Itineration is to be a style *within* an appointment. That is, the ordained representative is to move about amongst the people. In other words itineracy is initiating ministry and going to where people are. To me one of the most impressive facts about Jesus in the Gospels is his movement toward all kinds of people in all kinds of needs. Buckminster Fuller once said that God is a verb. Maybe that was an intimation of a process theology, but at any rate Jesus, too, is verb-like.

From Jesus' ministry, as well as the long line of Hebrew prophetic heritage, the ordained ministry has a mandate to move out. The Good Shepherd seeks the lost, exemplifying the God who searches for us and remembers us even when we have forgotten our own true life. In my own ministry I have seldom if ever regretted giving priority to being with people, either intentionally or by impulse. There are two cautions here: one is that our absence of a sedentary style should not be an escape from the vigorous demands of study and sermon preparation. The other is that it should not be a way of promoting our own needs to be seen or to escape the gifts of solitude that can refresh and re-create us.

The outreaching nature of Christian ministry is not optional. Rather it is basic to the Good News itself. If we lapse into the ease of a sedentary style of ministry, we have abandoned the ministry of Jesus Christ. The imperative of a sent ministry is a burden for our comfort and complacency. But what a blessing to our instincts to join Christ and his people in the intersections of life! And what an opportunity for ministry!

6. *Cosmic Implications: Intersection of the Local and the Global*

A distinct feature of ordained ministry is the universal or global implication. Increasingly I have come to believe that ministry should be done in the context of a global perspective. When we say that the whole world is our parish, we mean more than the responsibility of witnessing to the gospel in all places and cultures, as terribly important as that is. We are also saying that ministry is part of a global tapestry and that our work is informed and nourished by the worldwide Christian community. We are caught up in a story larger than our own, namely, God's drama of redemption/liberation for the whole world. This global dimension is almost entirely lacking in many forms of so—called secular work but is part of the anatomy of Christian ministry.

How can we minister apart from remembering the struggles and sacrifices of Third-World Christians across the world today? I cannot forget the saga told by a woman from Zimbabwe during the liberation struggle in which she described the loss in her country of virtually all outer forms and freedoms taken for granted in our daily ministry—the right to travel, freedom of speech and of assembly, the use of church buildings and nearly all financial resources. She closed her message by saying, "All we have left is the faith of our members." Do we pray for Christians in Northern Ireland? Do we do ministry in the light of Steve Biko? Do we remember the Boat People of Vietnam?

Do we see the face of Jesus Christ in the starving people of the world? Do we know that we are sustained by countless sacrifices of the past and of the present on ~ global scale? Are we capable of assimilating a broader theological context from Third-World people?

These events and images and many others like them today and in every generation connect us with the universal Lord and with a kaleidoscopic variety of persons and places. These influences enlarge our vision and help to prevent a narrow reductionism by which we make idols of our own limited situation. Elie Wiesel, the Jewish writer and interpreter of the Holocaust, can say in spite of the longstanding Arab-Israeli animosity, "I cannot *not* think of the Arab refugees." Lord, grant us a global vision that transcends our own space, time, and comfortability! First Church in Midtown, U.S.A., is irrevocably linked with all points east and west, north and south. The global context of our work is part of the glory and the greatness of ordained ministry, as well as all ministries of the ecumenical church.

The church has few tasks more important than enlarging the memory, the awareness, and a sense of identification of its members with people and their conditions of life throughout the world, often including many in our own geographical area. A motivating motto of the Vincentian Order of the Roman Catholic Church can instruct the whole church: "Go to the poor, not because they need you, but because you need them!" If you are looking for a comfortable, well-protected arena for work, the demands of a cosmic commitment and the liberations thereby presupposed will become a relentless burden.

7. A Tradition of Archetypes for All Types

During the initial years of my ministry the term "tradition" was nearly always perceived by me as having a negative connotation. Images of Pharisees, scribes, and elders immediately flooded my mental screen. Besides, I was much too involved with "creative" innovations of ministry to get trapped in antiques of the past. Gradually I learned that while many things were new to my personal experience, the treasury of the church's tradition already included in different historical settings many of the experiments that seemed so new—liturgical dance, the use of varied musical instruments, and pioneering ventures in church architecture. I also learned that the most theologically and pastorally significant innovations in any age are likely to come from those who know their church history and the traditions therein.

Through the years I have come to appreciate a very different understanding of the meaning of tradition. A particularly helpful focus came from Sallie McFague of the Vanderbilt University Divinity School. She points out that "a person must get inside a religious tradition, be able to move around in it both comfortably and critically, love it and question it at the same time. . . . This is what formation is about—the settling of a religious tradition into the very flesh and bones of one's existence."[6]

In the above tradition is used in a very broad sense to be inclusive of the whole range of Christian teachings in Scripture, as well as the tradition of church history through the years. The formation of faith is an inevitable moving around both critically and comfortably in a tradition. By this process tradition is no longer experienced as a fence that walls out fresh vitality and redirection. Precisely the opposite! Tradition becomes the raw material out of which God gives a life story and a new future. Tradition is not a fence, but a gate to the future, with hinges from the past. In actuality a true sense of tradition provides *roots* from which a future may be shaped.

The historical and transcultural power of the Christian gospel is of course rooted in the tradition of God's revelation through Jesus Christ. But what is it about this story that has enabled it to penetrate the depths of the human condition? Why does this particular script, one among many, continue to unfold on a

49

global basis? Many answers can be given. I believe that one of them—often overlooked—is because the Christian story is deeply embedded in the most profound and ultimate human experience: Crucifixion/Resurrection.

C. G. Jung made extensive reference to "archetypal images" to describe the commonality of human experience and the basic truths by which humankind has lived. By no means his own invention, Jung borrowed his term "archetype" from classic sources. Anthropologists, psychoanalysts, and others have pointed to a variety of archetypes that seem to transcend cultures and historical periods.[7] Archetypes touch us with the root meaning of our experience.

The biblical narratives are frequently woven around archetype images. A key Old Testament example is the Exodus event. It is an archetype of virtually all human struggle for growth, identity, freedom, and responsibility, whether individual or corporate. We yearn for a new future, yet its uncharted risk in the wilderness drives us to consider the safety and routine of Pharaoh's fleshpots. The dialectic of all freedom and responsiblity is a variation of this narrative.

If we theologize deductively, we begin with the premise that Jesus Christ is Lord and deduce meanings from that presupposition. But if we proceed inductively by looking at human experience, we will see that it is because the Jesus Christ story is the very metabolism of our experience that it has lasting power and meaning. The good in life is forever being defeated and reborn. We are forever saying no to life and then being grasped by a yes. Life is constantly coming out of death and new beginnings emerge from our endings. And this crucifixion/resurrection comes to us as an invitation to die in order to be reborn. This is the pulsebeat of human experience. Because the anatomy of the gospel tradition/story is the anatomy of life itself, the gospel is an inescapable truth about life for us all.

THE ANATOMY OF ORDAINED MINISTRY

On the global scale we as ordained ministers bear the Archetype Word in all types of human conditions and cultures. When we sign up for ordained Christian ministry, we have cast our lot with involvement in both the depths and the heights of divine and human experience.

For Reflection and Discussion

1. What other burdens and blessings not mentioned in these first two chapters seem to be basic to the ordained ministry as you experience it?
2. If you were beginning your ministry anew, what counsel would you give yourself and why?
3. How do you go about sharing these issues with one or more colleagues in the ministry in a way that encourages community and support for each other?

Chapter 3

MINISTRY FORMATION:
THREE INTERSECTING CIRCLES

Some time ago I had occasion to be in Pittsburgh. As is my custom when there is time in an unfamiliar large city, I explored the downtown area. What is "the feel" of the place? Where are the historic sights? What do expressions on people's faces reveal? What are the varieties of architectural forms? And where is the nearest Japanese restaurant, especially hibachi style?

On this particular Saturday-morning self-directed tour I was especially fascinated with the setting of the First Lutheran Church, the first English-speaking Lutheran Church west of the Alleghenies. When the building was initially completed in 1887, it dominated the landscape. Today it is dwarfed by business and industrial powers. The Porter Building crowds the church on the left. On the right, seemingly almost touching the church, Bell of Pennsylvania towers even higher. And across the street is the gigantic metal and glass edifice of United States Steel.

As I gazed at the once dominant church building now squeezed in between corporate giants, I wondered if this were a symbol of the church's relation to modern society. Then I crossed the street and wandered into the sanctuary. The coming Sunday was to be the fourth in Eastertide. I picked up the Order of Worship. The pastor's sermon for the next day was titled, "Look at All This Power." My curiosity worked overtime the rest of the day. I'll never know what backed up that sermon title in the next day's preaching, but I do know I have reflected a great deal since that time on the power and authority of the church and its ministry. In this chapter I hope to lift up a clue to the formation and authority of Christian ministry.

For me this clue is offered by Paul in his first letter to the church at Corinth. The fourth chapter begins: "This is how one should regard us, as servants of Christ and *stewards of the mysteries of God*" (I Cor. 4:1, italics mine).

As I note elsewhere in these chapters, Paul is all but obsessed with a recurring conviction that God has broken through conventional human wisdom in Jesus Christ, indeed, has reversed the world's accepted conventions. In the preceding Corinthian chapters Paul weaves this theme into the center of his message of the Suffering-Sovereign Lord.

The wisdom of the wise is destroyed and the cleverness of the clever is thwarted (1:19). One must become a fool to become wise (3:18). God has chosen what is foolish in the world to shame the wise; what is weak to shame the strong; what is low and despised to bring to nothing things that are (1:27-28). For Paul all of this has a sense of marvel and mystery that shakes the foundations of all human activity and achievement.

What it adds up to is this: The ultimate mystery of the universe is that the Suffering Lord is the Sovereign Lord who rules the world with grace and truth. The Vulnerable Lord is the Victorious Lord whose love cannot be destroyed, whose love is the only guarantee of life.

I believe this mystery of the Suffering-Sovereign, Vulnerable-Victorious Lord is the taproot of Christian ministry.

The Fountainhead of Ministerial Functions

When clergy are asked, "What do you do?" we are likely to answer with a list of functions. When we think of ordained ministry, our minds tend to center on traditional roles expressed in our daily work. We preach. We teach. We counsel. We administer. Liturgist. Organizer. Ecumenist. Change Agent. Enabler. Equipper. The titles vary but the functions are more or less predictable, at least for those who serve in the local church.

In Corinthians Paul is suggesting that none of these provide the clue to our authority or our activities. The fountainhead of all the functions is in our *stewardship of the mysteries of God*. A fountainhead is the main source of something but in a more particular sense it is a spring that is the source of a stream. When you observe a spring, you are in the presence of a mystery. It simply wells up from the ground in a seemingly endless supply.

You won't find spiritual stewardship on the world's inventory of most *useful* activities or enterprises. But just because we are set in the midst of powers and a world that frequently seems oblivious and preoccupied, we should not be deceived into believing that the world is without need of the gospel.

Sometimes the power of a poet's vision calls home this truth with striking power. Listen to T. S. Eliot:

> Where is the Life we have lost in living?
> Where is the wisdom we have lost in knowledge?
> Where is the knowledge we have lost in information? . . .
>
> A thousand policemen directing the traffic
> Cannot tell you why you come or where you go.
> A colony of cavies or a horde of active marmots
> Build better than they that build without the LORD. . . .
>
> When the Stranger says: 'What is the meaning of this city? . . .'
> What will you answer? 'We all dwell together
> To make money from each other'? . . .
>
> O my soul, be prepared for the coming of the Stranger,
> Be prepared for him who knows how to ask questions. . . .
> Life you may evade, but Death you shall not.
> You shall not deny the Stranger.[1]

Or as Thomas Merton asserted in his autobiography, contemporary society suffers from "prejudices that devour the people who know nothing but automobiles and movies and what's in the ice-box and what's in the papers and which neighbors are getting a divorce."[2]

As ordained ministers of the gospel our taproot is not in any function we perform but in the mysteries of God for which we are called to be stewards. This fountainhead of all our functions is our one and only authority. It is the essence of the Lord's Largess to the Easter People.

A Three-Dimensional Stewardship for the Mysteries of God

In the New Testament we see the diversity of gifts and graces given to the disciples through their experiences with Jesus. Although the first followers of Jesus were not persons of letters, so to speak, they were introduced by Jesus to a very intensive exposure of learning. For something like three years they listened to Jesus in all kinds of settings as he expounded on the reign of God and its meaning for their lives. More importantly, they saw God's reign in the life Jesus lived, and in his death and resurrection.

In the third chapter of Mark we are given this picture: "And he appointed twelve, to be with him, and to be sent out to preach and have authority to cast out demons" (3:14-15). This brief scene summarizes with considerable accuracy the events transpiring throughout the Synoptic Gospels between Jesus and the twelve.

To be with him. When we put that under scrutiny, two facts seem evident. One is a relationship characterized by prayer, expectant watching and waiting, and an inward searching in community. The wilderness or desert experience of momentary disengagement from the world was given birth for future Christian practice in Jesus' own example. In today's language we would speak of disciplined devotion, solitude, and meditation. Jesus and the disciples constitute a community whose wellspring is reliance on a transcendent yet always present God.

A second fact also seems clear. To be with Jesus was to get an education in the Old Testament and in Jesus' reinterpretation of the law. The disciples had their minds stretched and their values reoriented through a theological/ethical tradition shared in parables, stories, and proclamations. There are of course marked differences as well as similarities in Jesus' teaching and preaching in the Synoptic Gospels but in each work the reign of God is proclaimed and moral instruction offered.

To be sent out to preach and have authority to cast out demons. "Come unto me" is inevitably followed by "go into the world." The disciples receive more than training in spiritual discipline and in understanding and reinterpreting a tradition. They are sent on mission. More often than not the tasks of preaching and healing are the marks of the mission. Luke's narrative is particularly concerned with the disciples' mission. For example, Luke 9:1-2: "And he called the twelve together and gave them power and authority over all demons and to cure diseases, and he sent them out to preach the kingdom of God and to heal."

In Luke 10 we are told of the mission of the seventy. Their task is to heal the sick and to proclaim the nearness of God's kingdom (v. 9). Detailed instructions are given for the carrying out of the task. The mission emphasis is especially dominant in the Easter narratives, not only in Luke but in all the gospels. The key concern in which the Risen Lord is interested in all of the Gospels is the carrying out of the Good News of God to the present world.

If we assemble these learning experiences of the disciples in the Gospels, we discover something very close to three interrelated areas: *a spiritual discipline* (times of prayer, reaching inward, reflective thought and being with God and each other in a community of sharing); *knowledge* (including Old Testament passages, reinterpretation of Old Testament law, and reign of God ethics); and *the practice of ministry* (preaching, casting out demons, feeding the multitudes, and making new disciples). If we translated the experience of the disciples of Jesus into gifts and graces for ministry today, it would look something like diagram A.

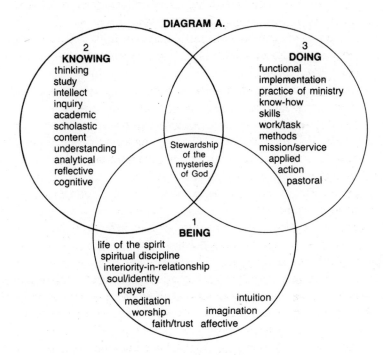

DIAGRAM A.

2 KNOWING
thinking
study
intellect
inquiry
academic
scholastic
content
understanding
analytical
reflective
cognitive

3 DOING
functional
implementation
practice of ministry
know-how
skills
work/task
methods
mission/service
applied
action
pastoral

Stewardship of the mysteries of God

1 BEING
life of the spirit
spiritual discipline
interiority-in-relationship
soul/identity
prayer
meditation
worship
faith/trust

intuition
imagination
affective

Stewardship for the mysteries of God encompasses at least these three arenas of largess that God has given to the church. They are meant to be suggestive, not systematic. As indicated in the diagram, these gifts intersect and overlap and cannot really be separated, although they are distinguishable from one another. The faithful development of these gifts is the Christian's response to the question, "How do I love God with all my heart, soul, mind, and strength?" These interconnecting circles will be referred to occasionally in succeeding chapters, especially chapters 4 and 7.

Most Protestant seminaries are called graduate professional schools. The *graduate* component (Circle 2) takes seriously the importance of knowledge and its relationship to truth, as well as the formation of a discerning mind. To learn the tradition is to become familiar with a large mass of biblical and historical content and substance. In recent years renewed emphasis has been placed on the *professional* practice of ministry (Circle 3) through internships, clinical pastoral education, and a variety of field education settings. The first circle, the life of the Spirit, has been a neglected dimension in many of our seminaries.

The fact that intrigues me about this first dimension of our stewardship for the mysteries of God is that in many Protestant seminaries it is neither a traditional *academic* subject nor a traditional so-called *practical* subject. To be sure the reality of the life of the Spirit is embraced within the academic and within the functional, especially in the context of an ongoing Christian community and its relationships. But it is also true that coping with life and with ministry itself is more than knowledge (gnosis) and more than skills (justification by work). We are saved and renewed by grace through faith, not by knowledge or by works, in spite of the great importance of each personally and professionally.

As I listen to clergy colleagues, and as I listen within my own journey, I'm increasingly convinced that weariness and futility in the ordained ministry is often not *primarily* due to lack of knowledge or to lack of skills, although lack of either can erode one's confidence in self and in the practice of ministry. The more critical issue frequently is the question of depth and renewability of one's own faith.

Circle 1 in the diagram draws together what could be called "interiority-in-relationship." By this I mean a quality of inner solitude or awareness that manifests itself in the capacity for caring and enduring relationship with others through our faith in God. While faith or spirituality will reach out through social caring and action, it begins in the inner life of the soul in relationship with God. It shapes one's identity and opens us to relationship.

Gene E. Bartlett, in his book *The Authentic Pastor,* tells of a conversation between Emerson and Thoreau about Harvard, their alma mater. "Well," said Emerson, "I see Harvard now teaches all the branches of knowledge." To which Thoreau replied, "Yes, all the branches and none of the roots!"[3]

I have always been extremely wary of the spiritual in ordained ministers that is not informed by a sense of intellectual inquiry and a sound professional practice. I still am. But in more recent years I have also become concerned about an intellect and a functionality that are not nourished and re-created by a deep taproot of personal faith. In other words *all three* intersecting circles represent inseparable yet distinguishable gifts for Christian ministry and thus make up our stewardship for the mysteries of God.

As an ordained minister striving to be a faithful steward of the mysteries of God, I seek to be aware of my needs for growth theologically, functionally, and spiritually. A theological seminary will do well to be more than a school for scholars, more than a trade school, and more than a place for private religious experiences. The task of theological education is to combine profound spiritual formation with vigorous academic work and competent practice of ministry. Our stewardship for each of these gifts leads us into the mysteries of God.

The Mystery of Knowing

The search for truth unveils expanding mysteries, as suggested again in chapter 7. No student of the Bible can fail to be awed by the beauty and profundity of the creation stories, nor the mystery of unfathomable givenness. No thoughtful inquirer can explain how the Ultimate Word has been written in so many diverse places, conditions, and times. Can the greatest biblical scholars of all time unravel the puzzle of the Divine Purpose being revealed through the years by outrageous earthen vessels—from a fugitive wanted for murder to untrained youth to a motley crew of tax collectors, members of the local fishing industry, and characters of ill repute? Our minds can merely grasp the fact that we cannot fathom the unsearchable ways of God. To us is given the mystery of God's transcendent Incarnation, "the uncontrollable mystery on the bestial floor" ("The Magi," W. B. Yeats). The stewardship of the scholastic inquiry leads to reverence and humility.

Students of church history know that we are stewards of every sacrifice and every act of compassion, from Stephen to Mother Teresa, from Jerusalem to all points of the compass. Students of the sacraments know we are inheritors of God's mysteries in a way beyond our deepest intellect. When I was a pastor of a new congregation in the Dallas area in the 1960s, I began to be troubled by serving communion to small children. The Methodist *Discipline* was silent on the matter and I was unsure of a theological reason for administering the sacrament to those not old enough for confirmation. To me it seemed as though the whole matter was a mere picnic atmosphere for the children who were without proper preparation and understanding.

After several discussions in the Worship Commission, I suggested that we invite Dr. Fred Gealy to our next meeting for some theological reflection. Dr. Gealy, now dead, was at that time teaching at nearby Perkins School of Theology. Secretly, I thought he would support my position before the committee. He accepted our invitation, came to the gathering, and listened to our viewpoints. I expressed my concern that the children did not understand the Eucharist, thus raising the question for me as to whether or not they should receive it.

He looked at me for a moment in silence, and then asked, "Do you understand it?" It was like one of those questions Jesus asked the Pharisees. Either way they answered they were trapped. If I replied yes, then he would surely ask me to explain the Eucharist. Was I really prepared to do that? If I said no, it would sound like I hadn't learned a thing in three years of theological education!

Dr. Gealy's point was that grace always precedes understanding. And even our limited understanding merely underscores the depth of amazing grace and astonishing love. I came to see the Eucharist as the celebration of inclusion in a community of grace, a gift to all ages and conditions. While there may be good reasons for some traditions that do not administer the communion to the preconfirmed, I have been at home in serving the Eucharist to children ever since the meeting with Dr. Gealy. Most ordained ministers have had the opportunity of a theological education but the mystery of God's grace is thereby deepened, not lessened. For this mystery we seek to be spiritual stewards in mutuality with the general ministers of the church.

The Mystery of Doing

Mystery is not limited to the intellect. It also pervades the practice of ministry. When I painfully admit my own weakness and my resistance to the very gospel I proclaim, I get in touch with the mystery of God's power to work *even* through me. Yes, and *even* through *others* whom I have dismissed or secretly downgraded! And even when I am at my "best" in preaching or in some other function of ministry, there is in retrospect—if not at the time—an awareness that something or Someone—not me—was on the move. Is there any more mysterious and humbling experience? How could we even momentarily consider the task of ministry unless convinced that we are undergirded or sustained by a mysterious largess beyond our own knowing, measuring, or controlling? Always the question is, What is ours that we did not first receive? A steward of divine mysteries does not possess, but is possessed.

THE PEOPLE OF GOD IN MINISTRY

The Mystery of Being

If knowing and doing are mysteries, so is being. The Easter gift creates and re-creates the Easter people. Our life of the Spirit is the mystery of encounter with the living God, "the Spirit himself bearing witness with our spirit that we are children of God, and if children, then heirs, heirs of God and fellow heirs with Christ, provided we suffer with him in order that we may also be glorified with him" (Rom. 8:16-17). Encounter with God is more than "knowledge about," more than a code of ethics, more than skills and methods. It is participation in a Presence that calls for self-awareness and self-worth, yet in relationship to the community of faith and to the whole creation.

The mystery of being is the mystery of personhood. As Calvin insisted, to know God is to know oneself. To truly know oneself is to know God. For many years I have believed that the number one hang-up for ordained ministers who are seminary graduates is neither inadequacy of knowledge nor dysfunctionality in skills. Hang-up number one is inability to relate to our parishioners as a genuine *person*. Sometimes we create distance by parading our knowledge or by coming across as super-professionals. Our people want to experience us as persons who can be trusted, who can admit our mistakes, who can take some good-natured ribbing, who can rejoice in the talents of our people, and who love the gospel of Jesus Christ and enjoy life.

For several years the Association of Theological Schools in the United States and Canada (ATS) has been developing a Readiness for Ministry Project. This program is a carefully shaped design by which seminary students can obtain assistance in measuring their preparation and readiness for ministry.

One of the initial surveys asked a wide variety of laity and clergy to provide data on what they considered to be priorities for the young minister or priest. When are you ready for ministry? What aptitudes, attitudes, and skills are deemed most important? The replies are illuminating. The top category of readiness had to do with willingness to participate in ministry "without acclaim." The next two priorities had to do with integrity and character of the beginning clergy person. Only *then* were certain *skills*, such as preaching and pastoral care, mentioned.

What all of this tells us is that the *personhood* of the minister is of greater significance than anything else. Not that the other things are unimportant, but they are seen as derivatives of the ordinand's personal commitment.

There is no ordained ministry that does not proceed from the personhood of the pastor. When you leave the parish to go elsewhere, what will people remember? Above all else we should be remembered as deeply caring persons in whom the people saw a glimpse of the truth of Jesus Christ spoken and lived in love.

Genuine spirituality in Jesus Christ leads us to a more profound "being at home" with ourselves and with others. No amount of knowledge and no finely honed professional skills can substitute for basic human qualities in an ordained minister. The qualities are called the fruit of the Spirit by Paul: "love, joy, peace, patience, kindness, goodness, faithfulness, gentleness, self-control" (Gal. 5:22-23).

In *Making the Small Church Effective,* Carl S. Dudley strongly affirms the importance of a loving relationship between pastor and people:

> The most frequent personal frustration for the laity (especially in a small congregation) is the feeling that the pastor, hiding behind that professional polish, is not a real person. They want to know the person; that is their first priority.
>
> There is no substitute for the presence of the pastor. He or she is the tangible symbol of love.[4]

Also affirming these human qualities is a statement by Leslie H. Farber in the foreword of William F. Lynch's book, *Images of*

Hope. Referring to Lynch, Farber says, ". . . he possesses a stubborn affection for the sheer ordinariness of life—an affection which Martin Buber in his writings on the Hassidim called 'the hallowing of the everyday.' "[5]

O God, infuse all of your ordained ministers with this priceless gift!

The Lord's largess to the Easter people is an amazing bounty of heart, soul, mind, and strength. For these mysteries we are stewards forever.

What Keeps Us Going?

When I became convinced years ago that I was to enter the ordained ministry—which at that time meant ending my work with Continental Oil Company and entering seminary—I received many good wishes and no little counsel from family and friends. My Aunt Marie, whose loving candor was shaped by a profound Christian faith that struggled with years of ill health, spoke to the heart of the matter.

> I know that there are many rough places ahead of you. We're not promised ease and comfort or even happiness as the world knows happiness, but joy and peace and fruitfulness to all who dare live God's way. I am more and more convinced that very few of us actually know and experience what the early Christians knew and felt—that Jesus Christ is alive and available with power and grace to see us through anything life can do to us. I pray that he will help you to so experience him that you can make him real to others.

Who has served in the ordained ministry without times of despair and utter frustration? Who among us has not experienced the night of the soul? (Luther) The Reverend Ms. Liz Lopez Spence, preaching at a Consultation of Women Clergy, stated that in her first year of ministry she left the ministry five times a week and now had it down to once a week!

MINISTRY FORMATION: THREE INTERSECTING CIRCLES

In the valley of dry bones, what keeps us going? What compels us to stay with it when our best efforts seem to make no difference? What moves us to find a Braille Bible for an aged person going blind? To drive forty miles in the dead of winter to comfort the distraught? Why do we care about a transient for whom no one else has the time of day? What brings us again and again to preach the Word of God whether at times we feel like it or not? How can we interface with the suffering of the innocent as a way of life without being consumed? How? Why?

Many reasons can be given. Perhaps all of them have a claim on truth at a given moment. But beneath all our vicissitudes there is a fountainhead of grace. The ultimate and universal Mystery of the Suffering-Sovereign One, the Vulnerable-Victorious Lord, has seared an indelible mark in the marrow of our bones and in the inner citadel of our spirit. The Mystery has called us to be stewards of the Eternal, the unending story, the Word that stands forever. In the Who of that Suffering-Sovereign Mystery is our why, our how, and our what.

For Reflection and Discussion

1. In terms of the three intersecting circles, where do you assess your own strengths and weaknesses, both from seminary experience and now in the practice of ministry?
2. In the light of your reflection on question 1, how do you think your response would compare to the leaders of the congregation you serve?
3. The New Testament provides many clues and images of ministry, including its authority and formation. What images are most significant for you and how do you theologize with them? Is there a key text for you, as I Corinthians 4:1 is for me?

Chapter 4

SPIRITUALITY FOR O'HARE AIRPORT

In going ahead with the Jesus Prayer . . . aren't you trying to
lay up some kind of treasure? Something that's every . . . bit as
negotiable as all those other more material things? Or does the
fact that it's a prayer make all the difference?

As a matter of simple logic, there's no difference at all, that I
can see, between the man who's greedy for material treasure
. . . and the man who's greedy for spiritual treasure. As you say,
treasure's treasure . . . and it seems to me that ninety percent of
all the world-hating saints in history were just as acquisitive and
unattractive, basically, as the rest of us are.[1]

Zooey to Franny

Readers of *The Christian Century* will recognize a series during
each decade entitled, "How My Mind Has Changed." If you
were describing the changes in your own thinking during the
past ten years, what would that look like?

For me it would include a renewed consideration of Christian
spiritual disciplines and their implications for my life and for
the people of God in ministry. I have always believed that faith
needs reawakening and constant nurturing. Yet through the
years I have had some very Zooeyian reservations about what
many Christians have meant by the spiritual life. Probably this
came about because it so often seemed to me that those who
raised the biggest noise about "the spiritual" made it sound like
another form of gluttony. Not only that, but affection for the
spiritual seemed also to be frequently attached to either material
avarice or to paternal attitudes toward other races and classes.

During the course of my ministry I have of course come to

realize that *every* word and *every* experience in the life of the church have been corrupted at times in one way or another. If this fact becomes our excuse to dismiss the matter or to refuse to work for improvement, what would be left? Many in the church have eschewed evangelism because someone else has misused it. Others stay away from social action because someone else misappropriated that. The concept of grace can become—and has at times in the church's history—an excuse for passivity. Deeds have been turned into attempts to earn our own righteousness. Shall we thus give up the concept of grace and works?

Our task as people of God in ministry is to critique ourselves and the church on behalf of a faithful expression of the gospel. It is of course a copout to allow someone else's unfaithful (in our opinion) use of God's gifts to become our reason for neglect or refusal to act responsibly. In this chapter I invite you to rethink with me some of the gifts of a disciplined life of the spirit and their implications for Christian spirituality in our time. We will explore several tentative definitions, review some very brief historical background, and take a look at some contours of spirituality today. Then I'd like to suggest several spiritual practices that nourish my own spirituality.

Toward Some Interpretations of Spirit Language

Spiritual language is like an eel—very slippery. Authors use it to suggest everything from a specific form of prayer to a way of life. It can suggest a quality of life permeating all dimensions of our experience, or a disciplined approach to meditation and renunciation. There are varieties of monastic spirituality, and there are characteristics of spiritual formation and devotion in theological education and in the life of the laity. An eye on at least some of the history of spirituality and its practices in the church has helped me to formulate a threefold picture of spirit language.

The Three-Circle Definition. In chapter 2 I quoted this statement from Sallie McFague: . . . "a person must get inside a religious tradition, be able to move around in it both comfortably and critically, love it and question it at the same time. This is what formation is about . . . the settling of a religious tradition into the very flesh and bones of one's existence."

In this context the term *tradition* is used to include *all three* of the intersecting circles of ministry formation explored in chapter 3. Spiritual formation, or the development of spirituality, in this broadest sense embraces knowing, doing, and being, that is, all the gifts that God gives to the church and its ministry. In this definition spirituality is more than interiority, the inner search, personal prayer, or an outward and visible charismatic spirituality. Spirituality in this broad interpretation includes the intellect and the implementation of ministry.

Today it has become clear that spirituality is a term increasingly used for meaning or depth in all areas of life. I receive continuing education flyers promoting seminars on creation-centered spirituality, holistic spirituality, a spirituality of social justice, a spirituality of nonviolence, as well as seminars on contemplative forms of spirituality. In Christian history the word *spirituality* is perhaps more common to Roman Catholicism than the Protestant tradition in which terms like spiritual growth, spiritual, and spiritual devotions have been more frequently used.

The One-Circle Definition. Some writers define spirituality by what a person does with solitude, that is, the Christian's practice of prayer and meditation. Here spirituality is a "One-Circle" term instead of the "Three-Circle" term, to use the above terminology from chapter 3. In this sense spirituality has only to do with the discipline of the inner life in its personal relationship to God.

Spirit language has been used in so many ways that it tends to defy precise definition. I think of the One-Circle definition of spirituality as including such terms as the life of the spirit, the spiritual life, the inner life, and the discipline of the spirit. In other words these expressions more often than not are intending to convey the experiences of prayer, meditation, and contemplation in their various forms of expression. While these practices nourish and nurture the total life of the Christian, they constitute a more narrowly prescribed area of activity than the broad definition of spirituality. The latter would include not only prayer and meditation, but also the way we live all of our lives.

Shaun McCarty, a member of the Missionary Servants of the Most Holy Trinity, suggests that spirituality is the way we live out of our depths in all areas of life (Three Circles); that spiritual formation consists of all the *intentional* provisions for nourishing the life of faith, yet distinct from both the academic/intellectual and the pastoral/functional dimensions (One Circle); and that spiritual disciplines constitute the specific ways and means of spiritual formation, such as prayers, community life, and retreats.

An Expanded One-Circle Definition. A third shape of spirituality is suggested in yet other readings. This view is in basic agreement with the One-Circle definition except that it is not restricted to one's solitude or private spiritual devotion. Corporate or community worship and prayer would be thought of as part of one's spirituality. In this way of thinking a prayer group, corporate worship, and charismatic rallies are dimensions of spirituality.

While my own definition of spirituality is the Three-Circle one, I can make sense out of the One-Circle definition as long as it is in the service of all three circles, regardless of what vocabulary is used to describe it. If spirituality is divorced from theology and the practice of ministry, it loses its substance and orientation. We already have a Culture of Narcissism (Christoper Lasch) without feeding it further through a world denying spirituality. The occupational hazard of all spiritual discipline is an unwarranted overemphasis on "how am I doing" instead of centering on and celebrating what God is doing. Just as undesirable is a theology without spirituality. The former without the latter loses its fervor and vitality and tends to become a wooden scholasticism.

In order to look across a slightly broader landscape I have found it useful to develop some historical sense of the routes traveled by Christian spirituality, especially in the West. What follows is a highly condensed and selective outline of a few slices of our roots in Western spirituality. Since at least one-half of the history of Christian spirituality in an ecclesiastical sense has been characterized mainly by monastic spirituality, you will not be surprised at attention given to it.

Some Brief Historical Background of Western Spirituality

Until well into the Middle Ages the most predominant and recognized form of spirituality was, with few exceptions, monastic spirituality. Monastic history from a Christian standpoint had its origins in the desert hermits of the late third century.[2]

The hermits of the Egyptian desert, the best known of whom was Anthony, were the forerunners of a monasticism that was to spread throughout the Christian church, both East and West. In the West monastic spirituality became largely communal through the establishment of monasteries from Italy throughout Europe during the fifth, sixth, and seventh centuries. Although not a great deal is known about him, Benedict of Nursia became the patriarch of Western monasticism due to the influence of his rule for monastic life, first utilized at Monte Cassino in the sixth century.

Even a most cursory review of Western monasticism would be seriously deficient without mention of the remarkable saga of Irish monasticism and its contribution to learning, art, and worship.[3] In the sixth century students from the continent flocked to Ireland for monastic and scholastic training. For several centuries Irish monastics profoundly influenced the Christianization of Scotland and England and initiated scores of monastic centers throughout Europe. Irish monks and scholars, nourished by their own Celtic tradition as well as Roman and classical influence, contributed a unique legacy in the history of Western culture by their commitment to pilgrimage in European lands.

The rule of Benedict was a far more moderate discipline than most Celtic monastic practices and gradually gained adoption throughout the West. Although Benedict founded no order, his rule for monastic life was virtually the only code for monks for more than five hundred years and remains today as the principal backbone of monastic influence. It continues to inform the Cistercian order, an eleventh-century monastic reform. Cistercian spirituality attempted to return to a pure, austere simplicity under the leadership of Bernard of Clairvaux.

The eleventh and twelfth centuries were the peak times of monastic strength and influence. By modern standards the withdrawal "from the city to the desert" appears to be sheer escape from the struggles of humanity on behalf of a search for the saving of one's own soul, to say nothing of an unjustified elevation of celibacy and the ascetic life as "the way" to God. In addition monastic practices came to be involved with a considerable amount of misdirected devotion to relics, the promotion and even the sale of indulgences, and other abuses identified later by Luther in his "three treatises." However, in the context of medieval history, some monasteries did provide a continuity of culture and spirituality in a very dark and despairing world. From place to place monasteries became storehouses for art treasures and manuscripts, and aided in preserving the heritage of the science of that time. To a degree they were centers of cultural life and religious intercession for the world.[4]

71

Another chapter in Western spirituality was written in the thirteenth century with the rise of the mendicant orders of Franciscan and Dominican friars. While being very different in temperament, organization, and outlook from one another, these friars were similar in their initial dependence on alms, their emphasis on preaching, and their seeking out people instead of withdrawing from them. Their spirituality did not major in solitude or seclusion but in itinerant involvement with people. With beginnings in Italy (Francis) and Spain (Dominic), the mendicant orders spread throughout Europe. Except for these influences, the medieval spirituality that was "recognized" by the church was almost exclusively monastic spirituality.

From the thirteenth-century monasticism experienced a decline due to several factors. In one sense the history of monasticism parallels a great deal of church history in that its success sowed the seeds for failure. Too much power and wealth became obstacles to the very ideals of monasticism. Too much worldliness undercut the vows of poverty, chastity, and obedience. Too many untrained new recruits compromised the vigor and vitality of the monastic rule. These inward signs of decay and deterioration were joined by vast outward changes: political upheavals and revolutions; the rise of the Renaissance with its emphasis on humanity instead of God at the center and the accompanying popularity of nationalism and the secular spirit; the Protestant Reformation with a strong protest and disavowal of monasticism itself. It was sometimes said that the Reformation all but obliterated monasticism in northern Europe while the French Revolution did so in much of southern Europe. Not until the nineteenth century did monasticism begin to experience a European renewal and also come to the United States.[5]

Paralleling the Protestant Reformation in the sixteenth century, a new religious order within Roman Catholicism arose that was neither fundamentally monastic nor mendicant. The followers of Ignatius of Loyola, a converted Spanish soldier, formed the Society of Jesus (1540), later to become a worldwide order of great strength (Jesuits). Ignatius saw a unity between prayer and action and a union with God in both through devotion to the cross of Jesus. "In Ignatian spirituality, then, contemplative prayer is subordinated and ordered to the active and apostolic life.[6] Similar to some emphases of the Protestant Reformation in this respect, the Jesuits' concept of spirituality combined prayer with action and thus opened the door to a more complete Christian spirituality.

The reformers brought very different perspectives to Christian spirituality. Luther in particular emphasized that all work was a holy calling, thus eliminating the priestly vocation as a special spirituality of salvation. The monastic spirituality that had been dominant in the church until the Reformation was frequently a One-Circle spirituality majoring in prayer and various spiritual exercises. Protestant spirituality represented a move toward a Three-Circle spirituality in which faith was given back to the whole church as God's gift rather than being a priestly province.

The Protestant Reformation was of course a complex ecclesiastical, theological, and political reform. But it was also a spiritual movement that insisted on the Christ of Scripture at the center of Christian devotion. This spiritual reform gave rise to family prayer, the inner life of the believer, an unparalleled creativity in hymnody, and a missionary enterprise.

From the time of the sixteenth-century Reformation, the Bible and personal prayer have been integral to personal spirituality for Protestant clergy and laity alike, although it has more likely been called spiritual growth or strengthening of one's faith. Likewise, participation in corporate worship has been viewed as a cornerstone of faith development and renewal. The spirituality of the eighteenth-century Wesleyan movement was closely tied to joyful singing and small group gatherings. For John Wesley spirituality could not be separated from either intellectual love of God or social holiness. His was a Three-Circle Spirituality.

Not even this very brief glance of Western spirituality would be adequate without mentioning English and American Puritanism and German and Dutch Pietism. Puritan devotion ordered all life under God among the common people, while Pietism loosened up Lutheran and Calvinist orthodoxy into what Wesley later would call "holiness of heart and life."

Each Protestant denomination has developed its own particular tradition, style of spirituality, and methods of spiritual discipline through the years. Anglican or Episcopalian spirituality is closely connected with *The Book of Common Prayer*—which explains the furor and intensity of feelings in that body when changes in the Book of Common Prayer are proposed. Quaker spirituality is associated with equality, simplicity, community, and harmony. The inward journey of Quaker silence in worship combines the inner search with the testimony and presence of community. All in all, the varieties of spirituality and disciplines of the spirit through centuries of Roman Catholic monastic and religious orders and through the many Protestant denominations provide a great treasury and tradition from which to draw.[7]

Spirituality Today: Resurgence and Reawakening

The decade of the 1970s saw a revival of interest in spirituality and spiritual disciplines. Why is spirituality "in"; how is it manifested, and what can we learn from it? Here are some provisional probings.

Spirituality is "in" because increasing numbers of people in the affluent sector of American society are looking for "more" . . . more than isolation and throw-away relationships, more than technological waste, more than drugs (either chemical or electronic), more than a rationalism without moral integrity or compassionate warmth, more than the asphalt jungle and the daily chase, more than impersonal and dull worship experiences.

SPIRITUALITY FOR O'HARE AIRPORT

Spirituality is also "in" because increasing numbers of people in American society are looking for "less" . . . less than responsibility for a frightening and fearful world, less than the freedom of ambiguity in a world rife with rapid change, less than facing up to the hard social issues that will not go away, less than toughening it out with ordinary people who don't have a mystic's view of community rapture.

In other words spirituality is "in" for all kinds of reasons, ranging from escape from hard issues to engagement with the world on new and deeper terms.

The resurgence of a concern for spirituality is manifested in several ways:

1. The sale of books concentrating on spirituality and mysticism during the 1970s and the beginning of the 1980s. The books range from a spate of spiritual narcissisms to the popular but probing works of the late Thomas Merton and of Henri J. Nouwen.

2. An increase in the use of retreat centers. Roman Catholic retreat centers all over the United States have reported full calendars, even a demand at times in excess of capability in terms of time and space. One of the newer activities of some monasteries heretofore virtually forbidden to public engagement is the training of nonmonastics in spirituality. Protestants, too, have caught the vision of a renewed spirituality, both in Three-Circle and One-Circle forms.

3. The widespread involvement of white, middle-class youth in Eastern religions, especially the practice of various forms of spiritual discipline under religious guides and gurus.

4. An increase in enrollment in higher education courses on various forms of Eastern and Western spirituality.

5. The ground swell of the charismatic and new Pentecostal experience that has cut across denominational lines, and to some extent, socioeconomic levels as well.

Spirituality Today: Renewal and Reappraisal

In the past several years I have been reappraising my understanding of contemporary forms of Christian spirituality. In his book *Living Together Alone*, Charles A. Fracchia examines "The New American Monasticism." He describes the ferment and transition occurring in various settings. These include traditional monastic communities (Benedictine/Cistercian) and other communities (both Protestant and Roman Catholic) of prayer, study, and work, yet not necessarily rooted in the Western monastic tradition or under a historic rule. The changes, although varying considerably from place to place, look like this: openness to Eastern spiritual traditions; less dichotomy between desert and city, that is, more variety of engagement with those outside the community; in some cases equal rights for women; less clericalism and more human community, part-time membership or involvement; and growing cottage industries.

As we consider the life of the church today, are there values in the ferment of contemporary spirituality that cry for a hearing? Are there messages from the new monasticism, both Protestant and Roman Catholic, that could be translated into our lives for a deepening of faith and mission? The intention of some of the new monastics is summed up in this remark made to Charles A. Fracchia on one of his visits to their community: "Our aim is to leaven and revolutionize the church through what British theologian Rosemary Haughton calls 'creative subversion.' "[8]

Considerable testimony in church history suggests the dependency of the church on a creative minority, beginning with the first disciples. The historian Arnold Toynbee has remarked on the indispensable role of creative minorities in the survival of civilizations. The Reformation itself and the Wesleyan movement in eighteenth-century England are witnesses to this truth. Laying aside for a moment our areas of disagreement with monastic spirituality, whether ancient or contemporary, what directions are lifted up that seem authentic and life-giving? I believe that today there is a sign value in the new American monasticism, signs very much present in various dimensions of historical Protestant and Roman Catholic spirituality. For me it takes the following shapes:

1. *The Sign of Simplicity.* The ancient monastic vow of poverty can be for all Christians a reminder of our life for others. The church needs to travel with light luggage in order to be fit for its ministry of loving care and liberation. Our real feast is in our fasting for others. Simplicity has become a sign of the gospel in a world of diminishing resources and in a world where poor Lazarus is legion. The sign of simplicity radically calls into question the consumer-oriented value system of our society and of the church itself.

2. *The Sign of Sharing and Solidarity.* In the monastic community the brothers and/or sisters have vowed a life of faithfulness to the gospel as they conceive it. The common good is regarded as a higher priority than rank individualism at the expense of others. The church's most important asset does not appear on the financial statement but only in the people themselves and in those whom we are called to serve in every circumstance of life. Human resources are cherished and encouraged.

3. *The Sign of Silence and Mystery.* I'm impressed with the use of silence made by monastic orders. I need more sanctuary for "the still small voice" in order to be in touch with the living God. All of us have at least a fraction of the ancient hermit in us who needs time and space for solitude. Denizens of our hectic times need a portable monastery in our souls, a reservoir of God-consciousness and inner fortitude with which to engage a world that is increasingly pushing in on us and pulling us in every direction.

When I hear of seminary students who are practically paralyzed—or else become frenetic—by a few minutes of solitude, I have serious reservations about what kind of relationships they will establish in their ministries. Silence depends on a trusting relationship with God and with a corresponding confidence in God's capacity to be with us. The sign of silence is a needed sign of "poverty," that is, our need to listen, to hear, to discern. The sign of silence is a sign of our openness to the transcendent.

4. *The Sign of Disciplined Devotion.* The rule of life in the monastic order provides points of reference by which a recurring life of prayer takes place. We live by many "rules of habit" such as a time to arise, a certain number of meals per day, and certain daily or weekly tasks to perform. What does it mean to establish your own rule for a disciplined spiritual exercise in prayer or meditation? A mystic once said, "The winds of grace are always blowing but you have to know how to set your sail in order to avail yourself of the breeze." What sails do you set?

Sometimes we are turned off by the term discipline or disciplined, even when it is by our own volition. If this terminology is bothersome, we can use other language that points to the same reality. For example, it might be helpful to speak of spiritual practices or spiritual intentionals in referring to prayer and meditation. The sign of spiritual discipline or practice is a recognition of how easily we reject God's gift of life and how often we need to open ourselves to receive again.

5. *The Sign of the Desert-City Connection.* The path of retreat and return between desert and city is a choreography frequently narrated in the New Testament. In recent years I have come to accept it not just theoretically, but in actual fact in my own life.

I am grateful to see an increasing responsiveness of the new monasticism to the needs of the world in terms of actual risk and involvement insofar as that is the case. Traditionally monasticism has committed itself to prayer, study, and work. For monks this constituted a type of Three-Circle spirituality, although their work was cloistered work and their spirituality was essentially disengagement with society.

Even so, monastic communities remain as a sign of the need

for spiritual renewal and of the inevitable connection between desert and city. These thoughts from Protestant and Roman Catholic Christians feed my own:

> As Christ searches our souls for the marks of his cross and the furrows of his passion, for the signs of our own personal union with him and commitment to his standards, there must be some trace of solitude, renunciation, and the refusal to capitulate to the world. And it is this challenge which represents the continuing importance of the hermits and monks of the desert.[9]
>
> *Thomas M. Gannon*
> *George W. Traub*

> Who are the most sheltered from the real world—those who are glued to the television set or daily newspaper, or those who identify themselves with the helpless and the bereaved through intercessory prayer? . . . Immersion in the world can often lead to isolation not only from the real world, but from the real self and from God.[10]
>
> *Donald G. Bloesch*

> He who attempts to act and do things for others or for the world without deepening his own self-understanding, freedom, integrity, and capacity to love, will not have anything to give to others. He will communicate to them nothing but the contagion of his own obsessions, his aggressiveness, his ego-centered ambitions, his delusions about ends and means, his doctrinaire prejudices.[11]
>
> *Thomas Merton*

Spirituality for O'Hare Airport

While these are signs to be appreciated from monastic spirituality as noted above, the problem of translating them into the lives of the vast majority of Christians and into the life of the church is a formidable one. The fact that monastics have withdrawn from the hustle and bustle of everyday life indicates that they themselves were not able to find or develop those

79

values apart from their monastic vows and community. Their personal stories seem to bear witness to discovering the gifts of simplicity, solidarity, sharing, and silence *only* in the community life of a particular monastic or monastic-like order. This is not meant to be pejorative toward them but rather expressive of the dilemma of the rest of us if we are to experience the gifts of silence and disciplined devotion.

The issue is still more complex for the majority of ordained Protestant ministers. Because many of us are married and have families at home, our lives are enormously more complex than the lives of the celibate clergy. During the writing of these chapters the demands and responsibilities of the family have been constantly close at hand—trips to the dentist, basketball games, chauffeuring after school and to evening basketball practice, washing dishes, and taking out the trash. More importantly, add the informal time for enjoyment of these relationships, and the picture becomes quite complex!

All of this means that family clergy by and large simply do not have anything close to the luxury of time for personal prayer, meditation, and the various religious exercises of the contemplatives or even of noncontemplative celibates. Of course this makes it *all the more important* to establish family-oriented devotions and/or to protect some time for disciplined spiritual devotion, whether in prayer, reflective reading, or use of silence. In my experience, some of the substance and values of monastic spirituality, as indicated above, are challenges to translate but the style will of necessity be radically different.

Some years ago I came to the conclusion that for me Chicago's O'Hare Airport was *the* symbol of the complexity of modern life. Movement. Speed. Anonymity. The coming and going at O'Hare, the size of the place, the number of terminals, the absolute shock of seeing a familiar face all of a sudden in the current of humanity! I've told friends that if you want to provide someone with a glimpse of the diversity of the American people, go to O'Hare.

My discipline of the spirit and the broader spirituality that it fosters must of necessity take place in an O'Hare Airport world, not in a religious community set apart. For O'Hare is more than my complicated world. O'Hare stands for the whole world for whom Christ died and toward which Christian spirituality must direct my life.

For me spiritual discipline takes several forms. One is the practice of brief moments of silence in order to foster a "God-consciousness." Moments of silence and quiet in between appointments and decisions provide a momentary "stepping back" in order to reenter the task with a fresh perspective. Brother Lawrence might have called it "practicing the presence of God." Meditation in this way reinforces my identity in the Word.[12] It is an act of listening, receiving, and centering on God's Word and God's Presence. Frequently this centering time confronts my condition of placing my own life too much in my own hands, attempting to control my own future or to insure that it will happen in a certain way. In this sense the silence of "God-consciousness" serves a purpose similar to corporate worship.

In *Life Together* Dietrich Bonhoeffer spoke of prayer as a time alone with the Word, giving us a solid ground on which to stand and directions as to the steps we must take. Prayer, he said, is the readiness and willingness to receive and appropriate the Word that it might lodge God's Word securely and deeply in our hearts. Spirituality is not a spiritual treasure to be hoarded. It is the acknowledgment of a gift and a claim that transcends and outranks all other promises and demands. Spiritual discipline is to be the servant of a total spirituality, the way of disengagement in order to reengage.

Harvey Cox thinks of meditation as a miniature Sabbath. "Sabbath originally meant a time that was designated for ceasing all activity and simply acknowledging the goodness of creation. . . . It comes every week, inviting human beings not to strive and succeed, not even to pray very much, but to taste and know that God is good, that the earth and the flesh are there to be shared and enjoyed"[13] What would it mean for us to take seriously the Sabbath notion by observing a day of recollection and renewal, either on a Sunday or some other day? No work. No "oughta dos." No "gotta dos." Recollecting. Rejoicing. Giving thanks.

James C. Fenhagen gives us still another view of meditation in this definition: ". . . a way of life which seeks to cultivate a deep and ongoing awareness of the person of Christ . . . that is increasingly aware of both the depths in one's self and the depth in others . . . a vision of life permeated with the love of God."[14]

Another form of meditation for me is more directed through use of Scripture. This is usually in the evening near the close of the day. I have been convinced for years that most writers on spiritual formation have an early morning bias. I am not one of them and except for the themes involved, I would enjoy a late night Tenebrae service more than an Easter Sunrise Service. Let us night owls arise—but not early in the morning—and claim the light of the gospel for the dark night! At any rate I especially appreciate reading in the Psalms, in Isaiah, and in the Gospels and Epistles.

Protestant ministers do not take monastic vows but we do take ordination vows as a "rule" of our office or our function in the church. I have become convinced that John Wesley's Watch Night Service (a Renewal of Our Covenant with God) is a glorious and profound reflection of the abundant Christian life, founded and empowered by God's grace. With this in mind I have slightly revised the service and for some time have been using it as a weekly liturgical Rule of Life. I trust it might be a useful instrument for clergy and laity of many traditions.

The entire liturgy, especially the Covenant itself, repudiates a self-serving ministry and calls us to a self-giving ministry in which Christ alone is our reward. Thus, rather than being an order used annually or only on special occasions, this service can become the heart and soul of our spiritual discipline through more frequent and regular usage.

The Order of worship which appears in *The Book of Worship for Church and Home* is itself the result of various modifications and revisions since its original form and use in the eighteenth century.[15] The changes in my revision are minor, consisting mostly of slightly reducing the length of the service in order to increase the feasibility of its regular usage in a period of ten to fifteen minutes. It can be combined with Scripture lessons from a lectionary and with meditation for an Order of about thirty minutes. I have retained the corporate or plural pronouns and the responsive nature of the liturgy in order to emphasize a global and timeless community, although this Revised Order can be used by individuals as well as groups. Without changing the basic meaning I have in places altered the phrasing to reflect an inclusive language. However, I have retained Wesley's use of thee and thou and other expressions of his time in order to preserve a historical continuity. The basic format of Adoration, Thanksgiving, Confession, and Covenant remains unaltered. I invite you to join me in the regular use of this Wesleyan spiritual service, or with modifications suitable to your own inclinations.

A Wesleyan Rule of Life

A Revision of Wesley's Watch Night Service for Regular Renewal of Our Covenant with God

Almighty God unto whom all hearts are open, all desires known, and from whom no secrets are hid: Cleanse the thoughts of our hearts by the inspiration of thy Holy Spirit, that we may perfectly love thee, and worthily magnify thy holy name; through Christ our Lord. **Amen.**

Dearly beloved, the Christian life to which we are called is a life in Christ, redeemed from sin by him, and through him consecrated to God. Upon this life we have entered, having been admitted into that new covenant of which our Lord Jesus Christ is mediator, and which he sealed with his own blood, that it might stand forever.

On one side the covenant is God's promise to fulfill in and through us the promise declared in Jesus Christ, who is the author and perfecter of our faith. That this promise still stands we are sure, for we have known God's goodness and grace in our lives day by day.

On the other side we stand pledged to live no more unto ourselves, but to God who loved us through Jesus Christ and who called us to serve in Christ's love that the purposes of his coming be fulfilled.

Let us then, remembering the mercies of God and the hope of our calling, examine ourselves by the light of God's spirit, that we may see wherein we have failed or fallen short in faith and practice and, considering all that this covenant means, may give ourselves anew to God.

ADORATION

Let us adore the God of love who created us;
who every moment preserves and sustains us;
who has loved us with an everlasting love, and given us the light
    of the knowledge of divine glory in the face of Jesus Christ.

**We praise thee, O God; we acknowledge thee to be the
    Lord.**

Let us glory in the grace of our Lord Jesus Christ;
who, though he was rich, yet for our sakes became poor;
who went about doing good and preaching the gospel of God's
    righteousness;
who was tempted in all points like as we are, yet without sin;
who became obedient unto death, even the death of the cross;

who was dead, and liveth forevermore;
who opened the way, the truth, the life to all believers;
who sitteth at the right hand of God in glory.

Thou art the Lord of glory, O Christ.

Let us rejoice in the communion of the Holy Spirit, the Lord and
Giver of life, by whom we are born into the family of God,
and made members of the body of Christ;
whose witness confirms us;
whose wisdom teaches us;
whose power enables us;
who waits to do for us exceeding abundantly above all that we
ask or think.

All praise to thee, O Holy Spirit. Amen.

THANKSGIVING

O God, the fountain of all goodness, who has been gracious to
us through all the years of our life: We give thee thanks for
thy loving kindness which hath filled our days and brought
us to this time and place.

We praise thy holy name, O Lord.

Thou hast given us life and reason, and set us in a world which is
full of thy glory. Thou has comforted us with kindred and
friends, and ministered to us through the hands and minds of
our brothers and sisters.

We praise thy holy name, O Lord.

Thou hast set in our hearts a hunger for thee, and given us thy
peace.
Thou hast redeemed us and called us to a high calling in Christ
Jesus.

85

Thou hast given us a place in the community of thy Spirit and the witness of thy Church.

We praise thy holy name, O Lord.

In darkness thou hast been our light, in adversity and temptation a rock of strength, in our joys the very spirit of joy, in our labors the all-sufficient reward.

We praise thy holy name, O Lord.

Thou hast remembered us when we have forgotten thee, followed us even when we have fled from thee, met us with forgiveness when we turned back to thee. For all thy long-suffering and the abundance of thy grace.

We praise thy holy name, O Lord. Amen.

CONFESSION

Let us now examine ourselves before God, humbly confessing our sins and watching our hearts, lest by self-deceit we shut ourselves out from God's presence.

O God, who hast set forth the way of life for us in thy beloved Son: we confess with shame our slowness to learn of him, our reluctance to follow him. Thou hast spoken and called, and we have not given heed; thy beauty hath shone forth, and we have been blind; thou hast stretched out thy hands to us through others in need, and we have passed by. We have taken great benefits with little thanks; we have been unworthy of thy changeless love.

Have mercy upon us and forgive us, O Lord.

Forgive us wherein we have wasted our time or misused our gifts. Forgive us wherein we have excused our own wrongdoing or evaded our responsibilities. Forgive us that we have been unwilling to overcome evil with good, that we have drawn back from the cross.

Have mercy upon us and forgive us, O Lord.

Forgive us that so little of thy love hath reached others through us, and that we have borne so lightly wrongs and sufferings that were not our own. Forgive us wherein we have cherished the things that divide us from others, and wherein we have made it hard for them to live with us, and wherein we have been thoughtless in our judgments, hasty in condemnation, grudging in forgiveness.

Have mercy upon us and forgive us, O Lord.

If we have made no ventures in friendship, if we have kept in our heart a grievance against another, if we have not sought reconciliation, if we have been eager for the punishment of wrongdoers and slow to seek their redemption.

Have mercy upon us and forgive us, O Lord.

This is the message we have heard from God and proclaim to you, that God is light, in whom there is no darkness at all. If we walk in the light, as God is in the light, we have communion one with another, and the blood of Jesus Christ cleanses us from all sin. If we say we have no sin, we deceive ourselves, and the truth is not in us. If we confess our sins, God is faithful and just, and will forgive our sins, and cleanse us from all unrighteousness.

THE COVENANT

And now, beloved, let us bind ourselves with willing bonds to our covenant God, and take the yoke of Christ upon us. This taking of Christ's yoke upon us means that we are heartily content that he appoint us our place and work, and that Christ alone be our reward.

Christ has many services to be done; some are easy, others are difficult; some bring honor, others bring reproach; some are suitable to our natural inclinations, and temporal interests, others are contrary to both. In some we may please Christ and please ourselves; in others we cannot please Christ except by

87

denying ourselves. Yet the power to do all these things is assuredly given us in Christ, who strengthens us.

Therefore let us make the covenant of God our own. Being thus prepared, let us now, in sincere dependence on God's grace and trusting in the promises of Jesus Christ, yield ourselves anew to God.

O Lord God, who hast called us through Christ to be partakers in this gracious covenant: we take upon ourselves with joy the yoke of obedience, and engage ourselves, for love of thee, to seek and do thy perfect will. We are no longer our own, but thine.

I am no longer my own, but thine. Put me to what thou wilt, rank me with whom thou wilt: Put me to doing, put me to suffering: Let me be employed for thee or laid aside for thee, exalted for thee or brought low for thee: Let me be full, let me be empty; let me have all things, let me have nothing; I freely and heartily yield all things to thy pleasure and disposal.

And now, O Glorious and Blessed God, Lord of All, Thou art mine, and I am thine. So be it. And the covenant which I have made on earth, let it be ratified in heaven. Amen.

For Reflection and Discussion

1. In your theology what is the relationship between corporate worship and a One-Circle Spirituality as defined in this chapter?
2. Where does the deepening and enrichment of your inner resources happen for you? Do you have a "Rule of Life" in relation to faith renewal?
3. As you define spirituality, what do you see happening in the church and in our society that is significant?

Chapter 5

MINISTRY, MEASUREMENTS, AND MADNESS*

Today there is a growing disparity in what constitutes the basic concept of ordained ministry. While some are moving rapidly toward the professionalization of ministry, others are increasingly suspicious of the professional model. Conflicting theologies of ministry are exemplified by statements like these:

> If the mission of the church is to permeate and mold the institutions of the world, then it could be said that a more devastating criticism of the church is not that it is professional but that it is not professional enough; that it is ingrown, mediocre, concerned with the wrong things, unwise in its allocation of resources and naive in its conception of the problems of modern man. In short, it is amateur.

> There is, I believe, something primitive, something romantic in Robinson's appeal to Paul the tentmaker as a model for the twentieth-century minister. What we need is a highly skilled, trained, intelligent articulate professional class which is in contact with the world and its center of power. We need a clergy that knows the world better than the world knows itself and that is able, therefore, to interpret this world so that Christians may be at home in it, act in it, love it, and take responsibility for it. And it is just because we do not have such a conception of the clergy that it is increasingly being regarded by the most thoughtful and idealistic young people as a vocation unworthy of their aspirations and abilities. They believe it is

*Adapted from William K. McElvaney, "Ministry, Measurements, and Madness. Toward a Theology of Ministry: Critique on a Unifying Image for Ordinands, Old and New and Yet-to-Be." *The Journal of Pastoral Care*, Vol. XXX, No. 1, pp. 55-68. Copyright 1976 by the Association for Clinical Pastoral Education. Reprinted with permission.

neither a demanding nor an influential means of service in the modern world. (A quote from Van A. Harvey in response to a speech by Bishop J. A. T. Robinson. Harvey's article, "On Separating Hopes from Illusions," was printed in *Motive*, November, 1965, pp. 4-7.)

JOB OPPORTUNITY — Lifetime — Hard work, low pay career as guide and servant-friend to people who are lost, poor, hungry, or burdened because they cannot find God, themselves, love, or their fellowman. Employer will furnish most essential tools of this trade, but Applicant must bring a supply of dedication, laughter, intellect, and a heartful of Hope you are willing to share with a world which has little of it. Your salary and compensation in the form of Gifts, left entirely to the discretion of your Employer. Apply to: JESUS CHRIST, c/o a Priest, Brother or Sister you know. (An ad in the *Kansas City Star*, November 9, 1974, sponsored by the four Roman Catholic dioceses in Missouri.)

. . . the confusion which surrounds the vocation of the ministry can be cleared away only by the creation of a new image. . . . What it means to be a professional person, known by high standards of education, skill, dedication, and institutional integrity, is the key to the new image. (Book jacket, *Profession: Minister*, James D. Glasse)

I would ask whether I am right in suspecting that an ideology of professionalism offers the governing paradigm. . . . I think the notion of the ministry as a profession is theologically ambiguous . . . as professionalization goes on, the image of the minister gets fuzzier. Defining the minister in terms of what the people want done makes him only the captive flunkie of the status quo. . . . (*Eschatology and Ethics*, Carl E. Braaten, pp. 147-48)

What are the most significant factors that impact ministry today? Many answers could be suggested. The momentum of women in ordained ministry. Ministry as lifetime learning through continuing education. Disenchantment with the political realm by the public, and a corresponding longing for a message of hope. Economic uncertainty. The gap between clergy and laity or between evangelicals and social activists. What others would you name? Surely one of the most influential factors has to do with the impact of professional knowledge and expertise from the behavioral and scientific fields. In this chapter I will examine this phenomenon as it relates to a theological critique of ordained ministry.

The Impact and Contribution of Measurements

In a way not heretofore embraced by the church—as far as I am aware—empirical resources are being brought to bear on ministry. The ministry is increasingly imaged as a profession in relation to other professions. As a profession the ministry can establish norms for competency, standards for excellence, means of evaluation, and resources for career assessment. The church is viewed as an occupational system with many component parts of the system (recruitment, placement, job analysis, role expectations, working conditions, remuneration, and retirement plans). In a sense, the church's ministry has discovered itself in relation to the modern world and has begun to utilize the expertise of business management, humanistic and behavioral psychology, and sociological research. All of this I am going to call the impact of measurements on ministry.

The phenomenon of ministerial measurements embraces at least two arenas. One is the dimension of professional standards for competency and excellence of practice. Included in this area of measurements are evaluation instruments in almost every ministerial relationship, such as minister-pastor/parish committees, and ministers-district superintendents, in The United Methodist Church. A multiplicity of forms for feedback is mushrooming, with evaluations covering performance appraisals and moving toward more complex and professionally offered career counseling and assessment services. Career growth resources are multiplying through continuing educational plans, and regearing of districts and conferences toward professional expectations.

Closely related to professional measurements for competency are matters related to ministerial support. If ministry is conceived as a profession, it means taking some new looks at salary structures, moving needs, and fringe benefits—in other words, the total church system in which the professional minister practices. Ministerial support also means ministry to ministers and their families through an expanding variety of counseling and support services. Programs vary greatly, but some examples are seminars for preretirement age; helping clarify expectations between congregations and potential ministerial appointees prior to actual appointment; retreats and seminars for clergy and spouses; and encouragement of peer or colleague groups for personal and professional growth.

The coming of measurements into the church recognizes the church not only as the Body of Christ but also as a human community with psychological dimensions, and as an institution with complex relationships. In my mind the utilization of measurements offers these contributions:

a) The use of data and research from other disciplines and a corresponding responsiveness to the complexities and needs of the church and the ministry today.

b) An emphasis on intentionality, management by design, and intelligent planning, both for members of the clergy and for the church.

c) A recognition of the importance of support structures and caring resources for ministers and their spouses and families. We are long overdue in enabling some vehicles through which ministers may give and receive care among themselves.

d) Motivation toward a self-awareness that is open to how others see and respond to what we are doing, and thus learning to develop trust in Christian community.

e) The synthesis, hopefully, of effectiveness and faithfulness in ministry.

MINISTRY, MEASUREMENTS, AND MADNESS

Donald P. Smith, in his book *Clergy in the Cross Fire,* offers this insight:

> The minister needs some basis for assessing what is actually happening as a result of his ministry. He may tell himself that this is unnecessary, since he is fundamentally accountable to God for *faithfulness* and not for *results.* Although he may find Biblical support for his position, he must also recognize in his ministry the calling to equip the people of God for the exercise of their ministry in the world. In this task, effectiveness is not easily divorced from faithfulness. The two dimensions are certainly not identical, but neither are they completely separable.
>
> Furthermore, the experience of both the Northeast Career Center and the Midwest Career Center seems to underline the human need of ministers to evaluate their ministry. Thomas Brown says that the major question asked by clients is, "How am I doing?" Similarly, Frank Williams finds recurring dissatisfaction among his clients because, with limited feedback from others, they find it difficult to know whether or not they are doing anything meaningful. Another counselor who has considerable experience with church personnel believes that one of the deep longings of the minister is for a feeling of competency.[1]

The concept of measurements in relation to ministry is of course not as new to theological education as it has been to the church-at-large. By the nature of the educational process (in this case, preparation for ministry), measurements in terms of grades or at least pass/fail systems have long been part and parcel of ministerial training. Some system of evaluation or measurement—whatever it may be—is virtually presupposed in education as growth, training, and preparation. Although the United Methodist *Discipline* prefers the term "ordained ministry" to the term "professional ministry," our schools of theology are known as graduate professional schools, with the emphasis in recent years being on the *professional.*[2] Seminaries

93

train candidates for the practice of ministry and evaluate those in training.

What is happening in the church-at-large today is that the concept of professional responsibility and accountability, already generally recognized in theological education, is now extended to the practice of ministry. To say it another way, we are now dealing with the questions, Why should candidates for ministry be expected to meet certain standards whereas once they have, so to speak, begun to practice ministry as appointed ministers or professionals, they are no longer responsible or accountable to their peers in ministry, or, for that matter, to the people whom they serve? Why should commencement of full-time ministry terminate measurements? Why should we have measurements to enter the ministry, but none to remain in the ministry?

In recent years I have more clearly seen that sincerity and piety are entirely compatible with gross incompetence, obscurantism, and a performance of ministry undeserving of the name "Christian gospel." In the name of calling ("my call is from God") we ministers can operate out of a grossly irresponsible individualism which is blind to the gifts and insights of our brothers and sisters in Christ. In the name of divinely given charismatic gifts we can seduce ourselves into thinking that we are above and beyond the evaluations of others in the Christian community. Deploying the transcendent as our shield, we can reject any self-exposure which asks us to hear the opinion of others, to be sensitive to the perception of others, to be open to a maturation process involving realistic notions of competent practice. As James D. Glasse forcefully puts it, "The assertion that one has a 'call to preach' is often taken as a license for irresponsibility. The call is used as an excuse for poorly prepared sermons, for pointless pastoral calling, for inefficient administration, for sloppy thinking, and for self-righteous social protest."[3]

One of the most promising features of measurements in

ministry today, that is, the concept of ministry as profession, is that it offers the hope of combining accountability of professional practice with the availability of care and support for one another. Rare is the individual who can fully function apart from some structure of continuing accountability. And rare is the individual who is not in need of the care and support of his or her peers in ministry.[4] Professional expertise may provide some handles on how we can care about one another. But I strongly suspect the motivation for caring in the church will most profoundly come from a deeper source than the professionalization of ministry. Which leads me to my next section.

Implications of Madness/Foolishness

I believe that professional "measurements" in the church are making a much needed contribution and that the use of diagnostic tools will continue. At the same time, some disturbing doubts are being raised about the meaning of the professional model. In my opinion these points of view need to be heard and to be held in creative tension with the pluses of the professional movement. This section of my critique will explore several questions about the professional emphasis, suggesting some reflections toward a theology of ministry based on a broader image.

In his book, *The Future Shape of Ministry,* Urban T. Holmes comments, "There are two dimensions to the church's ministry: the charismatic and the professional." The charismatic includes the contagious, the mysterious, the spontaneous, the eschatological. Note that "charismatic" in this connection does not refer to speaking in tongues, but rather to qualities and realities of experience which may defy measurements. Holmes also quotes Andrew Greeley's contention that "there is a dialectic element in the clerical vocation between the monastic and the secular."[5] It is the "dialectic element" in ministry which will receive attention in the following paragraphs.

95

In his address to the clergy in 1756, John Wesley spoke of the gifts and graces of ministry. Speaking of ministerial affections, Wesley insisted that a minister should "be endued with an eminent measure of love to God and love to all his brethren." He goes on to say that to go through all the toils and difficulties of ministry (inevitable in the office of ministry) without these loving affections would mean being utterly void of understanding, or like being "a madman of the highest order." A bit further in Wesley's *Address to the Clergy,* we read "he (minister) is ready to do anything, to lose anything, to suffer anything, rather than one should perish for whom Christ died."[6]

If I may reverse Wesley's pejorative imagery, "madness of the highest order" might also be a vivid description of one who is ready "to do anything, to lose anything, to suffer anything," that is, to be a fool for Christ. If competency for ministry is defined without reference to the absurdity of the gospel, without reference to the agape which is the touchstone of our ministry, and yet a scandal and stumbling block to the world, I begin to question, "Competency from whom and for what?"

I need to remember that most of our Lord's teaching—to say nothing of his deeds—turned the world's wisdom upside down. Is remembering this a problem for you, too? How does human wisdom, with all its managerial skills, deal with the Word that we are accepted as we are, and not justified by our excellence or achievements? How does humanistic psychology make sane sense out of a Word that teaches us to love our enemies and that the anatomy of human existence is the reconciling love of God which does not count our trespasses against us? And what does our human logic do with a Word that blesses the peacemakers in a society which provides accolades for those who make war? With a Word in which our "successes" may be failures, and in which our failures may be the birth of a new creation?

After all, Christian ministry is founded upon a gospel in which "God chose what is foolish in the world to shame the wise, God chose what is weak in the world to shame the strong,

God chose what is low and despised in the world, even things that are not, to bring to nothing things that are" (I Cor. 1:27-28). What if we surrender the foolishness/madness of the gospel in order to achieve a competence based on a conformity to the world's norms of excellence, in order to be effective according to the world's definition of effectiveness? Whatever became of those biblical images which defy human competence and ordering of life . . . Such as the first are going to be last, and the last first; the humble will be exalted and the exalted humbled; those who lose their lives for the sake of the gospel will find them and those who find their lives will lose them; every valley will be lifted up and every mountain made low? Whatever happened to God's plan, incompetent by the world's norms and utterly foolish by human conventions, of a crib, a carpenter, a crown of thorns and a cross, an empty tomb, a wash basin and a towel, a loaf of bread and a chalice?

These concerns are real to me. Perhaps my problem is that I'm not sure whether "competence" refers to what we do and how we do what we do, or whether "competence" also refers to why we do what we do, and from whom, through whom, and for whom. As Martin Luther King, Jr., expressed it, the world already has too many improved means for unimproved ends. Do competency norms measure ends as well as means?

I find a much-too-static definition of "calling to ministry" in many advocates of professional measurements. For example, James D. Glasse claims that "the call emphasizes *entry into the profession, not excellence in performance.*"[7] I would like to see "call" reinterpreted in more vital "process" terms to fit our actual experience—or at least my experience of call. For me, call to ministry has not been a once-for-all event in the past, as though once called, always called. Or called until no longer called. The call to ministry has been for me a recurring recreation, a recalling to ministry again and again. The recalling, at least for me, has been a call to faith and a call to perform ministry responsibly, intelligently, and competently.

97

Glasse makes the point early in *Profession: Minister* that a professional is identified, among other things, as a responsible man (person), a dedicated man (person), and an institutional man (person). These are useful categories from the professional model but I can just as well assert that these categories are constitutive of the gospel itself. I'm for obtaining all the help we can from professional insights, but since when do we need to borrow from sociological categories to figure out that we are supposed to be dedicated! If we haven't already heard that message from the gospel, and if we don't draw deeply from that well, I doubt that borrowing it from other sources can create much of a lasting stir!

Are we dedicated and responsible because we are professional or because we are grasped by the gospel and because we love the gospel! I think back over the many times when my ministry seemed too hard to perform, and too demanding for my energies. What sustained me in those times? What got me going again? For me it wasn't the idea that "I'm a professional and as a professional I'm dedicated and responsible." What it was—and is—is the Word—the gospel—the transcendent call and gift of God to ministry in the world. Perhaps my experience is not valid for others. But if it is, I believe that while the professional image should be an informing image in our theology of ministry, it cannot be the transforming reality out of which we function.

As Carl E. Braaten expressed it, "a musician may learn to compose, but that does not put music in his head." He goes on to say, "We need a theological doctrine of the ministry by which we can decide whether winning or losing, whether success or failure, is better under the conditions of church life in America. There are times when you can only win by losing; that is the lesson of the cross in history . . . a sound theology of ministry alone can free a person whose identity is not reducible to the sum total of the functions he has learned to perform in the interest of existing structures."[8]

Another concern I have about the professional image has to

do with the relationship of a profession to the public. One of the traditional attributes of a profession, according to some writers, is that it represents skills which society highly desires. In relation to ministry I see this as a half-truth. If ministry were desired by the public—or even by the church—as, say doctors and lawyers, ministerial salaries would be two or three times what they are. I believe that we do a disservice to the understanding of ministry to be constantly comparing "our profession" with "their profession." Certainly we stand to learn from other professions and their way of doing things—education, acountability, methodology, and the like—but always with one eye and ear cocked toward the New Testament message so that any "translations" which are made are not accommodations to a gospel-less competence.

What I am suggesting is that the desire for ministerial services rooted in the gospel is ambivalent in a way that is not true with respect to attitudes toward other professional services. True, people do not usually want to go to a doctor, and sometimes do not want to go to a lawyer. However, they do utilize their services and pay sizable fees. As ministers of the gospel all we have to do is look at the cross to be reminded of the fact that people do not want the gospel even as they want the gospel. The remarkable story of the Gerasene demoniac in Mark 5 is instructive—when the demoniac was healed and in his right mind, the whole neighborhood begged Jesus to leave immediately and sooner if possible! I'm not suggesting that it's a badge of honor to be asked to leave. I am suggesting that the whole gospel is both a sentence of death and a summons to life, and that we'd do better as ministers to see ourselves primarily in relation to the New Testament message than to the worldly status of other professions. For what other profession as profession has in its center a Suffering Servant? A crucified Messiah? An empty tomb? A Wordeed of irrepressible Grace?

Another potential danger in the professional model is that it can easily discourage the priesthood of all believers. I realize that the intention of a well-honed ministerial professional stance is the empowerment of the *laos*. Care needs to be taken, however, that the minister not become a professional whose skills are practiced "on" his/her people. If this becomes the transaction between minister and people, the professional model becomes an opiate encouraging passive dependence, and the people become like clients who are "acted upon" by the skilled professional. We are well aware, are we not, of the professional "aura" or mystique which can surround the professional person. If the impact of ministerial professionalization creates further distance between clergy and laity, it will surely be a loss to the church.

Whether or not professionalizing the ministry will embody the Divine Discontent with the status quo or promote ecclesiastical security for the most ambitious remains to be seen. If professionalization of the ministry fosters a ministerial syndrome similar to some existing organizations in other professions, we will not see the emergence of an advocate for the innovative and the inclusive. We will see instead a hardening of ministerial arteries. The more "professional" some professions have become, the more reactionary and resistant to fresh air! These observations are not intended to overlook in any way the high morality of individuals in the various professions, or the stated ideals of those professions. However, the actual institutional functioning of professional organizations does not, in my opinion, possess a stunning track record of creative change and openness to the poor and the oppressed. Nor a propensity for the kind of exemplary foolishness revealed from Bethlehem, Nazareth, and other unlikely locations. With the same to be said of the church's record, God forbid that any movement should erode our commitment to human liberation. And especially so under a euphemism of excellence!

Robert K. Hudnut, in *Arousing the Sleeping Giant*, is convinced that we are choosing the wrong models. We use organizational models that we are comfortable with instead of

6 2 0 2 0

the Suffering-Servant model. If it is true that Christians are those who follow Christ, then it follows that a church is not a church until it gives itself in suffering love. Suppose we use this analogy with the ministry. How are we going to evaluate, in our standards of professional competency, who has been faithful in suffering love? How can we do a performance review on agape? I raise the questions not to discredit the value of evaluations and competency standards, but to remind myself and others of the limits and shortcomings of such instruments of measurements. We must evaluate the evaluations from the standpoint of the gospel!

One of the most challenging tasks before the church today is to upgrade and strengthen our performance of ministry without falling into the trap of what Herbert Marcuse in *Eros and Civilization* calls "the performance principle" . . . making gods of production, promotion, and prestige. As I have reflected on our present situation in church and society, the more I have become convinced that for me the image of a liberated ministry is prior, but not inimical to a competent ministry . . . liberated for God's absurd agape . . . liberated for community with my brothers and sisters in ministry . . . liberated to accept gifts of others in ministry, whether male or female, Anglo or Third World, as basically complementary instead of competitive. What a church that would be! Liberated for my share of failures and goofs. (I wonder if our high-gear emphasis on competence instead of love, care, hope, joy and responsible freedom will trigger a whole new set of neurotic syndromes related to compulsive success standards and doing things the right way.)

Each person can draw on his or her own models or guidelines for what would constitute a liberated ministry out of which competence and excellence might flourish. Perhaps my worries are groundless, but I have an uneasy feeling that, if we grow competence apart from liberation of the self vis-à-vis the gospel,

101

we will experience an ingrown, self-serving and dysfunctional ministry.

Does the professional model tend to obscure the transcendent basis of ministry? How can the function of the prophetic make sense in the customary cultural professional model? While we need to affirm a theology of ministry informed by psychology, sociology, and anthropology, we need also to recognize that the wellspring of ministry is the transcendent Word Become Flesh. If the minister is just like any other professional, what has become of the notion of the prophet, the poet, the healer, the shaman? Does not the minister of Jesus Christ become least effective when he/she conforms to the prevailing social norms? Will a sense of the holy come through standardized norms? Whatever our conclusions, I believe these are the questions we need to be asking.

A Profile of Synthesis

If ministry is thought to be only a profession, we are almost sure to fall victim to a jaded and jaundiced view of our ministry, seduced by a professionalism characterized by craving for prestige, status, and standing in the church—in short, losing our transcendent calling and trading it in for ecclesiastical whoring. On the other hand, if ministry in the name of calling is resistant to intelligent and planned growth, to measurements through professional insights, we will in all likelihood render a defensive and narrow ministry, failing to develop our gifts for ministry which God has given us. It is the madness of the highest order that keeps the professional instinct Honest to God and Foolish for Christ. It is the advent of measurements in today's Christian community, which if closely hitched to the gospel, can usher in a more effective, more creative, and, yes, a more faithful ministry.

The synthesis of measurements and madness in ministry

takes seriously theological norms which are basic to the church. Madness of the highest order remains open to the unpredictability of transcendent grace and judgment, and the primary inspiration of Scripture. The presence of measurements—competency norms, standards of excellence, viewing the church as an occupational system—affords appropriate weight to the reason and experience of our historical epoch. Specifically, our way of acting and reflecting in ministry needs to take into account the historical and cultural differences in church and society today with the first century or New Testament era. Today we are dealing with a multifunction ministry, local churches with complex administrative requirements, transient urban and suburban populations, and a knowledge explosion beyond all previous historical experience. These factors—and many others like them—call for the importing of knowledge from various fields of experience, for the upbuilding of skills, and for a keen knowledge of how institutions function and interrelate. We do not betray our New Testament foundations by learning and coping with the specificity of the present age. Indeed, God calls us to do just that—but in the context of God's absurd foolishness!

To effect a synthesis of measurements and madness, of the professional and the prophetic, presupposes an openness to grace by which the Word is renewed in our lives. Only the grace of God's foolishness can ward off the otherwise inevitable advance of a culture religion which is finally joyless and self-righteous. Indeed, it is God's grace which provides the courage and freedom for competence, and for the openness required for evaluation, growth, and feedback. We know that the biblical Word is God's Word because it hurts too much and heals too much to be anything else.

In my own ministry I have found the phrase "speaking the truth in love" to be infinitely worthy of reflection and emulation (Eph. 4:15). For me it has been this "growing up into Christ" concept which links the professional and the prophetic. I commend its implications to the contemplation of ordinands new and old.

Speaking the truth in love might well be a cardinal motto for our ministry. To speak the truth in love is to intend the well-being of the other as imaged by the mind of Christ. Conversely, to speak the truth without love, that is, as a method of put-down or revenge, can be very destructive. Truth motivated by love means that persons are of ultimate significance, that issues of veractiy have importance only because they significantly affect the lives of people. Those who forget this often begin to justify almost anything in the name of truth or of "the mission."

On the other hand, for many ordinands the difficulty we encounter is that we begin to believe that we can love people without regard for the truth. That is, we try to love people without speaking the truth. We may establish long-lasting relationships, we may never lose any church members, we may endear ourselves as popular clergy. But without the Word of Truth which afflicts the comfortable as well as comforting the afflicted, we will not love people in a Christian sense, or, for that matter, in a biblical sense. We should thank God that God loves us enough to disturb us! How can there be resurrection without crucifixion?

One of the central reasons we need to be in close touch with biblical material and with feedback from those around us is to receive all the insight we can on how we are juggling and struggling with "speaking the truth in love." Truth without love turns the audacious into arrogance. Love without truth turns agape into sentimentality. Measurements and madness can be held in creative tension through the linkage of truth and love since this is the heart of the gospel itself. There are no simplistic rules to tell us when our "truth and love formula" is out of kilter. But we do know that there is forgiveness. There is feedback possible. And there is the God-given capacity for growing sensitivity toward the love and truth of Jesus Christ.

To speak the truth in love with our words, our deeds, our total lives is to embrace both the prophetic and the professional dimensions of ministry.

A Unifying Image of Ordained Ministry

One of our problems with the professional model today is that the original meaning of the term "profession" has become almost totally obscured. Apparently the word "profess" comes from the Latin prefix pro, meaning, "forward," "toward the front," or "into a public position," and fess, which derives from the Latin fateri and means "to confess, own, acknowledge." Originally a profession may have indicated "a personal form of out front public acknowledgment." That which was acknowledged or confessed (until about the sixteenth century) had to do with religion.

Gradually the concept of profession took on a more limited meaning and came to be used primarily to refer to the knowledge and skills possessed by practitioners of specialized traditions such as law, medicine, and divinity. "Thus the poles of meaning around the image of profession shifted from the proclamation of personal dedication related with transcendent principles to membership in and mastery of a specialized form of socially applicable knowledge and skill.[9]

A similar view of "profession" is that "the concept 'profession' is derived from the adjective 'professed' which has reference to vows taken by a religious order. The term was secularized by the seventeenth century . . . the 'learned professions' were identified as law, divinity, and medicine. In a historical sense there is no ambiguity about the ministry as a profession."[10]

I believe that ministerial morale depends, in part, on a creative balance between measurements and madness, diagnostics and discipleship, charismatic and professional, monastic and secular. The unifying image of ministry which speaks to me is precisely this creative balance.

Thus, the minister is one whose deepest intrinsic identity, whose primordial and primary image is the Word of Jesus Christ, as informed and influenced by a contemporary professional posture. Perhaps in this unifying image there will be re-presented the ancient professional meaning of ministry: "Proclamation of personal dedication related with transcendent principles."

For Reflection and Discussion

1. How do you view the use of measurements in the church as far as being either dangerous and/or positive?
2. Should the ministry as a calling or the ministry as a profession receive our greatest attention today, or should it receive equal emphasis? How would you theologize about your choice?
3. Would you support continuing education requirements for the practice of ministry? If so, how do you see the requirements being established and maintained?

Part II

THE MINISTRY OF ALL CHRISTIANS:

The Lord's Largess

Chapter 6

THE LISTENING CHURCH

The number of hotel guests waiting in line for breakfast seating far outnumbered the available tables. Finally having been seated at a table for two, I suggested to the waiter that the empty chair could be used in the light of so many persons standing in line. Soon another breakfast seeker was ushered to my table. In between placing our orders and downing our juice and eggs we managed one of those air-flight-like conversations. He was in Boston for a convention of specialists concerned with hearing problems; I for the semiannual meeting of the Association of United Methodist Theological Schools.

I have learned not to disparage these encounters, whether across the breakfast table, on a one-hour flight, or during one of those many waiting occasions that are part of life's coming and going. Momentarily we enter the life of another human being, and they ours. The similarities and yet the endless contrasts of our lives! Wherever we travel, whether in the United States or the far corners of the globe, is there ever any sight as truly absorbing as another human life?

Before we went our separate ways my breakfast companion shared some memorable information. Researchers in a university, he told me, have been engaged in testing the hearing level of entering students over a number of years. If I understood him correctly, the research indicates that twenty years ago 5 percent of the entering students had experienced some hearing loss. Today 65 percent have measurable hearing loss. While the degree of loss is usually not substantial at this age, the increased rate of hearing loss is alarming.

Three factors related to the student loss of hearing struck me with particular force: (1) the loss appears to be directly connected with the increased level of noise in our society; (2) most of the students are unaware of their own hearing loss; (3) the average age of persons in our society needing and obtaining hearing aids is much younger than in past years.

These cultural phenomena bear a message to the Christian church in our generation. The increased volume of noise in our society is both literal and figurative. Most of us who have teen-agers know the experience—if we have a family car—of the sudden and deafening blast of rock music that engulfs us at the ignition turn on. After several forgetful experiences of this kind, I have learned to check the radio dial *before* I turn the ignition switch. And why is it that my teen-agers prefer the TV volume much louder than their aging father who should be the one in need of multiplied decibels?

The noise level in our society, however, is more than a volume increase. It is an increase in cacophony, that is, "a discordant and meaningless mixture of different sounds" (*The Random House College Dictionary,* revised edition, 1979). If there are no clear sounds that call us to identity, no clarion notes that shape a life-center that stands above all the other sounds, then will not our identity become as confused as the cacophony itself?

As a number of authors have called to our attention, it was not by accident that the 1970s witnessed a renewed exploration of spiritual exercises designed to experience a focused or centered life. In *Turning East* Harvey Cox took the reader on his journey of examining and experiencing many facets of contemplation, chanting, and other practices of Eastern religions. "The dozens of masters and gurus I talked with taught me some basic tools for psychic survival."[1] Charles A. Fracchia introduces us to both Western and Eastern communities of spirituality in his book *Living Together Alone.* His conviction is that in a world of discordant and confusing noises, the "new monasticism is providing a leaven in contemporary society."[2] Or to put it otherwise, all of these means of spirituality are intended to serve as a listening device sorting out the cultural cacophony for the sake of a life commitment. This emphasis on listening is itself a reminder to others that loss of hearing may be happening without conscious realization and that we may need hearing aids as never before.

The First Act of the People of God in Ministry
"He who has ears to hear, let him hear." This admonition of Jesus appears in all three of the Synoptic Gospels. Hearing is a central activity in the New Testament. There is no discipleship that does not begin with the ear. Everything depends on hearing with understanding. Without hearing discipleship is stillborn.

Listen for a moment to the New Testament (italics mine):
Go and tell John what you *hear* and see. (Matt. 11:4)
The blind receive their sight . . . and *the deaf hear.* (Matt. 11:5)
Seeing they do not see, and *hearing they do not hear,* nor do they understand. (Matt. 13:13*b*)
Hear then the parable of the sower. (Matt. 13:18)
Hear me, all of you, and understand. (Mark 7:14)
Hear, O Israel: The Lord our God, the Lord is one. (Mark 12:29)
A great multitude . . . *came to hear him.* (Luke 6:17*b*)
Take heed then *how you hear.* (Luke 8:18*a*)
The dead will *hear* the voice of the Son of God, and *those who hear will live.* (John 5:25*b*)
You cannot bear to hear my word. He *who is of God hears the words of God;* the reason why you do not hear them is that you are not of God. (John 8:43*b*, 47)

Even this cursory glance reveals that hearing is the gateway to the gospel. Hearing is life. Hearing is heavy. And hearing is more than merely hearing. According to Jesus, true hearing involves understanding, reflection, perception, discernment, and commitment as response.

Martin Luther insisted that the gospel is always a matter of hearing. Faith is never a possession as though, "Now I've got it!" Faith is a gift that we accept and reject over and over again. Yesterday's bread will not suffice for today. We need a fresh supply! The circumstances of our lives are never exactly the same. Our spirits are up and down and somewhere in between. So the story of our lives is hearing the Story over and over again. Always again.

To listen is to be in a receiving position. Before the disciples knew what to do or thought they knew what to do or dared to do what they did not know how to do—they listened. Ears precede feet. To listen is to focus on what God is doing. If the church doesn't begin here and come back here, it has no chance of going anywhere. If the church does not receive the gifts of God, what has it to give to the world?

The Bible centers on God's initiative. Otherwise there is no gospel, no Good News. We may "do theology" by beginning with human experience as our point of departure. But our first and last point of reference is God's Word; otherwise we have no place to go from human experience except the human condition itself. Listen to the wisdom of theologian Karl Barth:

> The Bible tells us not how we should talk with God but what [God] says to us . . . not the right relation in which we must place ourselves to him, but the covenant which he has made with all who are Abraham's spiritual children and which he has sealed once and for all in Jesus Christ. . . . We have found in the Bible . . . not the history of man but the history of God![3]

To listen is to be in a receiving attitude. Receiving is difficult because it presupposes need, dependence, incompleteness. Humility is not one of the seven deadly sins although our society often teaches us the Male Macho Be Number One at All Costs Approach to Life. The poor in spirit are blessed in the

Sermon on the Mount because their basic posture is willingness to admit need. In other words they are open to listening and hearing, the indispensable prerequisite for being embraced by the gospel. Thus the "essential credential" for participating in the coming of God has nothing to do with merit or moral fitness. Whatever else we are as the people of God in ministry, we are first of all a listening people.

The Ultimate Therefore: Before and After

All Christian theology is therefore theology. Regardless of whether the starting point of reference is God's initiative in Jesus Christ as in classical theology or the people's experience of deprivation and misery as in liberation theologies, the theological steps will be traced to the Story. The key contours of the Story will be a journey from Eden to Exodus to Easter to Everyday life.

The Story for Easter People does not begin or end with Easter, but it does focus on this incandescent point. While we were yet sinners Christ died for the *un*godly. Therefore! "What wondrous love is this, O my soul! What wondrous love is this that caused the Lord of bliss To bear the dreadful curse for my soul."[4] While we were yet sinners, the Suffering Lord who was crucified became the Sovereign Lord whose way, truth, and life live forever. Therefore! While we were yet sinners the promise of God's indestructible and unconditional love was victorious. Therefore! While we were sinners, the claim of God's call to human dignity and social justice for all is forever made clear. Therefore!

Because God has embraced you with the promise and claim of Jesus Christ, *therefore* live your life accordingly. *Therefore,* respond to life in ways that are appropriate for one for whom Christ died. And care for others for whom Christ died in a way appropriate. On the After Side of the Ultimate Therefore you belong to Christ. The most crucial decision in life is whether life is *my* story or *God's* story. If life is fundamentally about *God* and God's purposes in life and creation, then my story is part of a larger fabric of history and humanity. To be part of God's story is to be involved with a Word—Jesus Christ—that at times *heals* in such remarkable ways that it could only be God's Word; that at times *hurts* too much to be anything else but God's Word; that *hallows* life through individual relationships and through commitment to justice in structures and systems. The church's reason for being is to live out the Great Therefore in relationships and acts of caring.

To hear the Good News is to be touched by a mysterious love Who calls all life into being, yet is before us and after us; Who affirms our worth in spite of our failures, offering new beginnings to all our endings; Who undergirds the worst sinner with redeeming love and undermines the best Pharisee with judgment calling forth repentance; Who beckons us to risk for others, yet gives no worldly guarantee of victory other than the victory of risk-filled truth itself. Therefore!

Hearing Aids for Easter People: Designed

If the first act—indeed the ongoing response—of discipleship is to listen, to hear, to receive, how does God enable us to do so? How does God speak and what hearing aids are we given in the midst of cultural cacophony? Having ears to hear, how do we indeed hear?

Through the centuries the church has pointed to various means of grace that were given by which faith could be renewed and sustained. Through these means of grace the ultimate promise and claim of Jesus Christ once again encounters us and calls forth decision. The list varies according to whom is drawing it up, but we can point to some more or less commonly experienced hearing aids. For example Wesley, in his sermon entitled "The Means of Grace," asks, "Are there, under the Christian dispensation, any means ordained of God, as the usual

114

channels of his grace?" He then lists prayer, both individual and corporate; searching the Scripture (which implies reading, hearing, and meditating thereon); and receiving the Lord's Supper, as the usual or *ordinary* channels of God's Grace.

For Wesley "means of grace" meant outward signs, words, or actions ordained of God and appointed to be channels whereby God might convey preventing, justifying, and sanctifying grace. He insisted that none of these had any intrinsic or inherent power and were of no use apart from the Spirit of God. Agreeing with Luther, Wesley underscores that it is God alone who is the giver of every good gift, the author of all grace. In reply to his own questions as to how one could attain such grace and how one could come to believe in grace, he answers, "All who desire the grace of God are to wait for it in the means which God has ordained; in using, not in laying them aside."[5]

Here I would like to emphasize again, as suggested in chapter 4, the function of prayer as a hearing aid. While prayer may be speaking silently or audibly, it also is a means of listening. Many people find it difficult, if not impossible, to pray in the sense of addressing God at a particular time or place like Tevye the dairyman in *Fiddler on the Roof.* The Quaker tradition of "centering down" and listening to the Spirit of God, both in community and in solitude, can be a means of grace in which a deeper God-consciousness can take place. Perhaps we are too prone toward "talking prayers" and need to sit still in "listening prayers." Is it not true in human relationships that we are too often talking when we should be listening? A listening church is an Easter People in waiting, a people unafraid of the solitude of the desert, with sensitive ears to hear the Vulnerable/Victorious One in the midst of cacophony.

Reading, hearing, and meditating on the Scripture, like prayer, is a hearing aid given to both the gathered congregation and the people scattered. Whether corporate or individual, the Scriptures provide an anchor and a compass for our prayers and our contemplation. Since Vatican II the Scriptures have been given a more prominent place in the worship services of the Roman Catholic Church. Likewise, increasing numbers of Protestant churches now utilize both Old Testament and New Testament readings with the latter frequently including both Gospel and Epistle selections. Scripture is a cornerstone and touchstone of the people of God in ministry, providing content and substance to our consciousness, our life as a community, and our commitment in mission. More is said in the next chapter regarding the Scriptures as a source of learning for Easter People.

For me, the Eucharist or Lord's Supper has been a very powerful hearing aid through the years. In 1959 I was the originating pastor of a new congregation on the east side of Dallas. A layman on our Worship Commission suggested in the early 1960s the use of a common loaf for our Communion service. Since that time the Eucharist has never been the same for me and I must confess an outright bias on behalf of the common loaf over crackers, wafers, and tidbits! (See I Cor. 10:14-17.) I have come to prefer a common chalice for small groups and also for use by intinction with a larger group.

The Eucharist overwhelms all my defenses. The elements point to the largess and legacy of the Suffering-Sovereign Lord—unbounded, unmerited grace for me and for you. Is there anything greater than this? It is as though the whole universe is completely explained while at the same time it remains an utter mystery. Do you know what I mean? It is as though we are addressed as the unique individuals that we are but at the same time as members of a common community of humankind. Don't be surprised if you see me moved to tears of gratitude during the Eucharist, regardless of whether I am on the distributing or receiving end of the elements.

At Saint Paul School of Theology we have chapel services on Tuesday and Thursday mornings. Often these are rich experiences of worship. For me a recent Eucharist service turned into a feast of hearing and receiving in a totally unexpected manner. It is usually the act of distributing or receiving the elements themselves that deeply moves me in the service of Holy Communion. On this occasion, however, a deeper vision of what it means to be a theological administrator came to me as I was sitting in the pew *looking* at the elements on the communion table and participating in the liturgy.

I began to realize that I was *being asked* the question, "What does it mean for the desk in my office to become that communion table?" I began to see one superimposed on the other, so that the elements rested on the united form of the two. The loaf and the chalice touched everything on my desk and all the transactions that come across it. I knew that sitting behind a Eucharistic desk, I would never administer the seminary in quite the same way as before. I knew that every administrative detail and decision would in some way represent the hurts and the hopes of human beings, that the brokenness and wholeness of life would be at stake on this desk become table, that even roof repairs and HEW forms would point beyond themselves to the total task of the Risen Lord and the Easter People.

Perhaps the deepest experiences of spirituality and revelation, divine-human encounter—call them what you will—defy adequate theological analysis. When the scales fall off our eyes, who can explain it? When the ears of the deaf are opened, who can plumb the mystery? When awestruck, we can merely form a word on our lips: grace.

One of the church's most underrated hearing aids is baptism. Luther spoke of baptism as a lifetime challenge to live out. In times of doubt and despair he was sustained by touching his forehead and repeating the words, *"Baptismatus sum"* ("I am baptized"). Baptism is a visible proclamation that we are God's, that we are given a place in the Easter People, and that accordingly we are called to the ministry of outreaching love. It is a unifying bond between laity and clergy, indeed, reminding us that we are as needy infants before God and utterly dependent on the gift of grace.

117

We may not want to hear what baptism has to tell us. Is that why the church has so often relegated baptism to a neat and tidy occasion that belies its momentous meaning? We are not self-sufficient and we cannot save ourselves . . . we are not in control of past, present, or future and our lives are meaningless apart from God's unmerited gift of grace-filled love . . . there is no healing and hallowing of life apart from some hurting and risking . . . in the eyes of God we are no more important or valued than the mongoloid child or the bedridden out-of-sight crew at the nursing home on the outskirts of town.

We need to turn our baptismal hearing aids onto a higher volume so we can hear the message. Enlarge the fonts and stir up some waves as befitting the struggle of death to the old self and resurrection of the new being! Insist that the Easter People participate in the liturgy, concluding with a resounding amen! We are celebrating the grace of God, the initiation of a person into the Easter Community, and the ministry of all Christians to which we are appointed by baptism.

No God-given hearing aid had more prominence in the ministry of Jesus and the life of the Easter community from the beginning than preaching. "How are men to call upon him in whom they have not believed? And how are they to believe in him of whom they have never heard? And how are they to hear without a preacher? And how can men preach unless they are sent? So faith comes from what is heard, and what is heard comes by the preaching of Christ" (Rom. 10:14-15a, 17).

There could hardly be a clearer statement of the inseparability of the church, the Easter event out of which came a new People, and preaching. One can merely take a few Concordance phrases under the term "preaching" to get in touch with the priority of Jesus' mission and that of the New Testament church: . . . preaching in the wilderness of Judea . . . came into Galilee preaching the gospel of God . . . preaching in their synagogues and casting . . . preaching the gospel to many villages . . . preaching boldly in the name of the Lord . . . Macedonia, Paul was occupied with preaching.

Laypersons rightfully expect competence and a sense of urgency in the preaching of the Word. Along with pastoral care and possibly administrative duties, there is no task from week to week that requires the constant time and effort from a clergy person as does preaching preparation. Preaching is the heart and soul of the Easter People, the occasion when Jesus Christ the Crucified/Risen one confronts us anew with saving grace and life and death decisions. In preaching, the ultimate promise and claim come to us again, albeit out of past history and tradition and yet as a brand new event for life in the moment of hearing.

From time to time I correspond with Saint Paul graduates, especially several who were "second career" students when they came to seminary as was I. These words from one of them during her first year in the pastorate following graduation tell at least part of the story of every preacher:

> It was terribly hard to get my sermon. I never really got it, though I made about six outlines—all different. Finally chose one and preached it. The people listen so intently it frightens me. Some lean forward in the pews. It gets so still you could hear a pin drop. It's frightening, Bill.
>
> Last week I had a terrible time getting the sermon together. Finally, I got the outline together after dreaming that I was to preach it in a strange place outside—a big Christmas sermon. In my dream many people, all strangers, were to be there. Finally an old preacher came running up, spent, and lay on the platform. I went over to him and he said, "Just get up there and preach like you were God!" Well, I needed confidence, but really.

As one who has been on both the preaching and listening ends of sermons over a period of years, I offer three convictions about tuning up and tuning in our hearing aids for the hearing of the Word through preaching:

1. The receptivity of the hearers can be a magnetic force in

strengthening and enlivening the preaching. Black congregations have understood this well and thus work with their
preachers in a dialogical give and take during the sermon.
"Come on now. Tell the story. Don't hurry. Well. Don't hold
back." While this style might seem forced or even phony for
white congregations, it suggests the importance of preacher and
people giving birth to the sermon as a whole.

Once when I was preaching to a conference for three
consecutive evenings, several ethnic persons began to verbalize
encouragement during the first evening. My wife told me later
that she leaned over to the person seated next to her and
exclaimed, "We're going to be here for awhile." She knows me
well! The next evening at the beginning of my sermon, I told of
her comment, and went on to say that perhaps every
congregation should select an official "egger-onner" whose
chore would be to draw out the best possible sermon from the
preacher. The sermons might be longer but they would *seem*
shorter due to the increased vitality and excitement of the
preacher!

2. The listener is as responsible as the preacher for the
happening of the true and lively Word. Well, not quite, but
almost. True, an awesome responsibility rests squarely on the
shoulders of the preacher. There is no escaping the study, the
sensitivity, and the tenacity required in this audacious task to
which one is called. Yet the most faithful, creative, and
brilliant preacher imaginable cannot preach the Word into your
heart and soul unless that Word is given an open door of
anticipation and expectancy.

An analogy related to theological education may help
underscore the point. A great deal is expected of a theological
seminary and rightly so. I have indicated in chapter 3 three
basic areas of growth or formation in the training of ministers
and in the lifelong maturation that hopefully follows. However,
whenever the strengths and weaknesses of seminary curriculums
and programs are debated, we must also discuss the importance

of the individual student if we are to get an adequate picture of responsibility for theological education. No curricular improvement and no additional program emphasis in any area can substitute for the personal integrity, imagination, tenacity, commitment, and commonsense of the individual student. Not even genius in preaching can take the place of the listener's imagination and introspection as applied to the preached Word.

3. Sunday morning listeners should not expect an exclusive homiletical diet of smooth and comforting assurances. To be sure the gospel comforts all who mourn and offers a garland instead of ashes, the oil of gladness instead of mourning (from Isa. 61:2-3). But the same gospel condemns idolatry, rebukes those who want cheap grace, and carries woe to anyone claiming false righteousness. It is the responsibility of Easter People to make it clear to the ordained minister that he or she is to proclaim the *whole* gospel. I still recall the comment of a parishioner many years ago about my preaching. "Your sermons were sometimes hard to swallow, but always nutritious." It is the *responsibility* of the preacher to preach the whole story in love through sound biblical and theological preparation.

Though most Christians may not have thought of it in this way, the liturgy of the worship service constitutes a hearing aid by which the faith community can reappropriate the message of the gospel. The framework of the service, the call to worship, written or extemporaneous prayers, affirmations of faith, assurance of pardon, a children's time, the offering, the benediction—constitute what has often been called the great lay catechism or theological schooling for the laity. The great themes of Christian faith are held before us as the story we are to live in our life from day to day.

The Christian's life is a liturgical life, that is, the themes of liturgy compose a script that provides the contours of our existence—adoration, praise, renewal or confession, thanksgiving, and commitment to service and sacrifice. Thus, liturgy

121

as the work of the people is more than participating in the liturgy, and more than helping prepare the liturgy. God's gift of liturgical forms and styles provides the basic ingredients or themes that the people of God in ministry are to *practice* in daily life. The living out of the liturgical themes constitutes the work of the Easter People.

In most congregations music is an indispensable feature of the worship experience. I mention it separately because in my own life it has so often been one of those hearing aids through which the gospel has been reborn, on the feeling level as well as the spiritual and intellectual. I'm no musician but I learned long ago that music, both instrumental and vocal, can have a powerful influence on life. I cannot even imagine the church without its hymns and its repertoire of music through the centuries.

Hearing Aids for Easter People: Undesigned

To become a listening people is to identify the hearing aids that God has provided. So far we have focused on some of those means specifically given to the worshiping and waiting people of God. Wesley referred to these means of grace as ordinary or usual channels. We might call them "designed," that is, they are deliberately designated through Jesus or through church tradition for the faith renewal of the Easter People. For the most part these channels are directed to the corporate Body of Christ, although of course prayer and searching of Scripture are just as significant for the scattered people as well as the gathered people.

However, we know that the Word we celebrate and acknowledge in corporate worship is the Word by whom the world was made, who calls us into being, and who encounters us in all of life's experiences. Indeed, it is the hearing of the Word in worship that equips us to hear that Word in the vicissitudes of personal relationships, family life, occupations, politics, and all events of history. "God can convey His Grace," said Wesley, "either in or out of any of the means which He has appointed."[6] Luther declared that if God once spoke through Balaam's ass (Num. 22), God can speak through anything, whether stone, stick, or thunder!

As Christians we sometimes forget the implications of the biblical doctrine of creation. As Creator, God has been loose in the world since the very beginning. Indeed, the Gospel of John's first words are, "In the beginning was the Word, and the Word was with God, and the Word was God." For the Hebrews history was the arena of encounter with God. In the events of life God was revealed, speaking in judgment/mercy, establishing a covenant with the Israelites and leading them out of Pharaoh's bondage to a promised land by way of great struggle in the wilderness. In other words God was heard *in life*. Our Old Testament ancestors in the faith developed a vocabulary to describe what they experienced, issuing forth ultimately in Scripture, tradition, creeds, and songs.

All of this is to say that our ordinary hearing aids ("means of grace") in the life of the church point to what God has already done and is doing in life. We should not be surprised, then, when we hear God in daily events. Theologian Paul Tillich, in interpreting art forms, used to speak of "religious style, nonreligious content." By this he meant an art form that does not have traditional religious symbols or substance, such as Jesus and the disciples, yet has a religious style in that it evokes an ultimate concern or reaches beneath the surface into the depths of our lives. Maybe this can be a helpful clue in understanding how God speaks to us in the events of life. The real presence of God in Jesus Christ is not limited to the sacraments, sermons, or songs of the religious community. It is their function to point to the real presence in the ups and downs of our everyday existence.

So it is that God comes to us in a kaleidoscopic variety of

experiences. In moments of sorrow and tragedy our hearing aids often seem to be momentarily turned off and tuned out, or at least we experience so much static that we discern no clear message. Yet in our losses and disappointments God has a way of coming to us as companion and comforter. Have we not noticed how often it is that those who have known unusual trial speak not finally of bitterness but of gratitude for life's blessings? In the New Testament joy is never associated with favorable circumstance or outcome.

Many Christians have discovered their most profound experience of God in ministering to others through personal care or through a courageous stand for social justice. God can only seem real to us if our lives reflect a reaching out to the need of others. In the cries of our neighbor we hear God speaking. To listen and respond is to find ourselves as well.

In the midst of flight from self and life, who knows when like Elijah we will hear "a still small voice"? The voice of God in solitude. The voice of God in the whirlwind. God's means of grace are beyond our measurement and calculation. The ordinary means of grace in the life of the gathered church are meant to tune our ears to everyday grace in the world.

Indicators of Hardness of Hearing
Indicators of Receiving and Perceiving

How can we tell when our hearing aids are finely tuned? What are the signs when we are growing hard of hearing the gospel?

When we are able to experience our "wounds as occasions where God intimates a new creation" (Henri J. Nouwen), we are hearing the gospel.

When availability to the suffering of others becomes a higher priority than acquisitiveness of things, our ears are tuned in.

When we discover a growing social conscience and an insistence that the church make clear that Easter People are on the side of the powerless and the forgotten, the message is coming through.

When our economic and political opinions serve no greater cause than our own vested interests, we are having hearing difficulties.

If *anything* has become more important than faith working through love, we need a checkup on our hearing aids.

If we've allowed ourselves to become cynical and have no sense of expectancy about what God can do through committed people, hardness of the hearing arteries is setting in.

When our faith is expanded to a global concern and to an awareness of the universal Christian church, it is an indicator that God's Story is becoming our story.

When reconciliation overcomes alienation, the gospel is on the march.

When suffering is transformed into a deeper compassion for others, we have met the risen Christ.

When through Jesus Christ our failures become our building blocks instead of our stumbling blocks, the empty tomb is a fact of our experience.

When the means of grace cause us to stop lying to ourselves and to gain self-respect through a searing honesty, we are on the road to Emmaus.

When the Word we hear is not that of a successful superstar but that of an unsuccessful Crucified One who links our redemption with the liberation of others, we have ears to hear.

When the gospel frees us to make mistakes because we dare to get our hands dirty in linkage with lepers, somebody is doing some listening.

As people of God in ministry we will do well to ask ourselves, "What hearing aids has God given us that equip us to hear? What new acoustical gifts might God be trying to give to me?" Loss of gospel hearing tends to be fatal to Easter People. The open ear is the way to the open tomb.

For Reflection and Discussion

1. What "designed" and "undesigned" hearing aids are most important for you?
2. In what ways could the listening church become more faithful in your congregation, both for clergy and for laity?
3. As you read Scripture, ask yourself, "How is God speaking or revealing the divine purpose to human beings? How does God come into life? How does God become real?"

Chapter 7

THE LEARNING CHURCH

For many years two contradictory sayings have stood side by side in our society. The first saying is this: "You can't teach an old dog new tricks." The second statement: "You're never too old to learn." In the first church I served, I taught a weekly evening Bible class of some ten persons. Among them was an eighty-two-year-old woman named Austa Wyrick. She lived across the street from the parsonage and we got to be on friendly terms right away. But in the Bible class she said nothing until the third or fourth session.

After the class had finished that evening and everyone else had departed, she said, "Young man, I want to ask you something." With some uncertainty I indicated my willingness to hear. "In all the years that I've been in the church, why have I never heard before now an approach to the Bible that has helped me understand how it was put together and how to interpret it from the context of the passage itself?"

Austa Wyrick has been dead for several years, but she'll continue to live in my memory and ministry as an example of a learning church.

The learning capacity of the laity is the greatest single human resource of the church. In my own tradition of United Methodism the ratio of laity to clergy is approximately 300 to 1. This fact alone suggests the vast potential given to the people of God, to say nothing of the imagination, insights, and experience of the laity. At the outset of this chapter the reader should know that I am going to focus intentionally on adult formation or learning.

In recent years some denominations have moved toward greater accountability of the clergy, especially in regard to continuing education. An *ethos of expectation* has been developing by which clergy as professionals are expected to be involved in a lifetime learning process. Theological education is increasingly seen as the initial launching pad into ordained ministry with foundational knowledge, skills, and personal readiness for ministry. I like to say that unless you continue your education, your basic theological degree will self-destruct in three to five years. Doctor of Ministry programs have mushroomed into prominence within the last decade as a major component of continued learning. Continuing education units (CEU's) are given by seminaries and other educational agencies for non-degree courses and programs. Congregations are expected to provide sabbatical and continuing education time and funds.

Lay Accountability

In the 1980s the church will face no greater question than this: *To whom and for what is the laity accountable?* As we have moved in the direction of more visible clergy accountability, the church must likewise be laying the keel for launching an ethos of expectation for lay leadership. Accountability must be a two—way street applying to both clergy and laity unless we are content to develop a very unbiblical one-sided double standard of accountability and expectation.

How can church members become participants in responsible adult learning, especially our lay leaders who have responsibilities on boards, committees, and work areas? Why should we expect clergy leaders to be involved in lifelong learning unless we also expect proportionate learning from the church's lay leaders? While to be sure a great deal of learning takes place beyond formal designs of education, why should we expect the latter from clerical leaders and not from lay leaders?

THE LEARNING CHURCH

The future faithfulness of the church to the gospel of Jesus Christ is inevitably connected with the question of lay learning and accountability. Unless there is an imaginative and effective program of lay learning across the church, the consequences are usually predictable: we inevitably drift toward popular cultural assumptions; we become adjusted, acculturated, and adapted to a domesticated religion of benign spirituality; we lose the Divine Discontent of Christian thought and action. The constant "messages" of the society around us anesthetize us to the needs of a suffering world and the gospel is remade in our own image. In short, we lose the wonder, the challenge, the power of the gospel that calls us to be *trans*formed to Jesus Christ, not *con*formed to the world. Without lay learning on a vast scale, so called lay enablement will in actuality result in an erosion of historical and theological vision, a *dis*ablement of the power and authority of the Word in the Body of Christ.

In his book *The Seduction of the Spirit,* Harvey Cox reflects on the loss of people's religion. His words carry immense importance for our churches today.

> When a group loses its *corporate autobiography* (italics mine) it can quickly disintegrate into an amorphous aggregate in which personal interiority disappears.

> A people's religion includes . . . memory and nostalgia. It is a living compilation of the songs and ceremonies a people accumulates through its history, *a fund of remembrances* without which there could be no future at all (italics mine).[1]

Although in these statements Cox was thinking primarily of the religion of oppressed peoples, his insights apply to *all* people and religions. The withering away of common remembrances and the erosion of a sense of corporate autobiography causes us to emphasize our many differences rather than our mutuality in the faith, both between and within denominations. As this loss of memory, so to speak, continues to occur, the need for adult learning is increasingly underscored.

Twenty years ago James D. Smart wrote a book called *The Rebirth of Ministry*, (A Study of the Biblical Character of the Church's Ministry). In a chapter entitled, "The Teaching Ministry," he eloquently described the connection between a teaching ministry and an active discipleship, as well as the consequences of an untrained laity:

> The weakness of the church at many crucial points arises directly from this failure of members of the church to become disciples of Jesus Christ. It causes a tragic shortage of competent lay leaders because so few mature adults have any thorough education in the faith to which they are earnestly committed. Their Christian education ceased in their teens. They have read little or nothing about their faith (Although the sale of religious novels and religious books that are like spiritual get-rich-quick manuals is sometimes large, books that would be useful for growth in real discipleship have a pitifully small sale. . . .) The consequence often is that men become lay leaders in the church not because of any unusual development or competence or understanding of a peculiarly Christian nature but because of their eminence in their business or profession or because of their engaging personal qualities. They have the character of a leader, but not the knowledge or understanding or penetrating Christian judgement that are necessary to empower them for Christian leadership.[2]

Before turning to some ways and means for promoting a learning church, it will be useful to look at some barriers to learning that sometimes block our path.

If the learning church is to become more fact than fiction, the clergy must face up to our own temptations of possessiveness and paternalism. Too often I hear discouraging stories from laypersons detailing the inability of pastors to engage in mutual ministry. If clergy want an educated laity, we need to be willing to teach, to share, to become mutual learners. We should be at least as concerned with the continuing education of our laity as with our own. We need to plan for the learning process with laypersons so that mutual growth can take place for the benefit of the church. In other words, the attitude of the pastor in relation to lay learning and growth can either put a ceiling on the potential or else maximize the waiting-to-be-fulfilled-gifts that God gives to the faith community. If we as pastors don't get excited about the growth of our laypersons, to say nothing of our growth together, what are we doing in the ordained ministry?

As a layperson, are you willing to risk new learning and are you willing to work at loving God with your mind? That's the other side of the coin—and I've heard some discouraging stories from pastors on this count. Too many laypersons, we are told by seminary graduates, have their minds set in concrete. There is little willingness to explore or to experience new knowledge or insights. Reinforce the past and keep all other opinions to yourself!

The church has a right to expect the training of all lay leaders in basic biblical interpretation, theological reflection, and the ministry of all Christians. It is not the expectation of learning that is unreasonable or too demanding. Rather it is the expectation that a high standard of lay leadership is possible when no training occurs in the basic areas of the church's life and faith for which leadership is expected. Without a laity in learning the alternatives before us are clearly a church dominated by uninformed laity *or* by clergy through lay default! Does anyone really desire either of these alternatives?

Fear of Learning

We all must wrestle with the fear of learning in order to experience breakthroughs toward a learning church. Several years ago I decided that I wanted to enroll in a continuing education course in some field other than theology or seminary administration. Accordingly, I poured over the avalanche of continuing education offerings received in the mail from area colleges and continuing education agencies. I considered a wide range of possibilities from yoga to karate to auto mechanics to Chinese cooking. Finally, I narrowed the list to two possibilities: Spanish or piano.

For many years I've had this fantasy of being a master of the keyboard, capable of enthralling an audience with daring and original improvisations. So I signed on for eight private piano lessons at the Jewish Community Center in spite of barely knowing where to find middle C. The lessons began in October. By November I began experimenting in *The Methodist Hymnal* on our piano at home and made a covenant with myself: I would learn to play "Joy to the World" by memory by Christmastime. After several weeks of endless and rotelike repetition, my wife was wishing I had opted for Spanish!

Soon I tried a few measures of "Joy to the World" for my instructor. He nodded with a benign smile but suggested that I not play too much of "Joy to the World" at this location (Jewish Community Center). Thinking he was surely being overprotective, I tried a few additional lines the next week. This time the door of the room swung open and a young attendant motioned for my teacher to step into the hallway. When my teacher returned, he informed me that the policy of the Center prevented certain selections of music. As it turned out later, following a conversation with the Center director, the matter was straightened out. The attendant had simply overreacted when hearing my tune as he walked down the hallway near my lesson room. When I later told our seminary chapel organist about the episode and the temporary consternation that it caused me, she replied, "Well, at least you played it well enough that they recognized what it was!"

Today, "Joy to the World" is all I play, although I gained a new appreciation and respect for the years of training and discipline that go into making a musician. At times I felt foolish and embarrassed, especially when the student whose lesson immediately followed mine was a thirteen-year-old who made the piano come alive with melodic sounds. And made it look simple in the process! The most important learning from the experience was the fact that it's O.K. to feel foolish and embarrassed in the service of attempted new learning. And this is terribly important for adults to discover because the fear of feeling or appearing foolish—or stupid—is one of the great deterrents to adult education. If our selfhood is rooted in Jesus Christ, we don't have to impress others or worry about "getting it all together." [God] "is the source of your life in Christ Jesus, whom God made our wisdom, our righteousness and sanctification and redemption; therefore, as it is written, 'Let him who boasts, boast of the Lord' " (I Cor. 1:30-31).

When Jesus Christ is our center-of-being, our animating principle and person, we are freed to learn, to risk, to discover anew, and to feel foolish in the process if need be. When Jesus Christ is the final Word for our lives rather than our own ego, learning assumes a joyful and anticipating face instead of a fearful or anxious one. In the previous chapter I emphasized the listening church as a dimension of the Lord's largess and thus "an essential credential" for the ministry of all Christians. If we hear the Good News of God's love and perceive ourselves as part of that ongoing cosmic and global story, our lives will be set free and will thus take on a future-oriented posture for God's mission in the world.

For me the challenge of new learning sometimes leads to an initial feeling of discouragement because I have to come to terms with how much I don't know. But then there comes a wave of exhilaration in the excitement of new knowledge and the possibilities that it heralds. To love God with all of our mind is, in the strength of Jesus Christ, to welcome new facets of our Christian tradition.

Fear of learning comes from theological concerns as well as psychological. Sometimes seminary students fear that theological education will attempt to explain away the mysteries of God and thus destroy their faith. On the contrary, intellectual inquiry and new learning are not keys to unlock the mysteries of God. Mystery on *this* side of disciplined knowledge may be a euphemism for ignorance and intellectual laziness. Mystery on the *other* side of knowledge is a knowing that hallows life and that profoundly convinces us of the sovereignty and the *ingenuity* of God! Knowledge has deepened my devotion, not decreased it.

To learn the intricacies of Bible development—the oral transmission, the varying purposes of the authors, the historical context, and even the contrasts and conflicts—does not diminish God's revelation to humankind. Precisely the opposite! The years of biblical formation prove the wonder of God's *ingenuity* to work through earthen vessels of virtually every description. My own theological education was and always will be a major watershed of thought, inner change, and reconstitution. These years of intense learning did not decrease my sense of the majesty of God; they increased the wonder of God's mysterious ways.

Scientists in our day are speaking of the *mystery of the known.* Awed as we are by what we apparently do not know, it is the enlarging framework of the known that instills reverence and amazement for the expanding scientific mind. Astronomer Carl Sagan has said that our sun is just one of two hundred billion stars in the milky way galaxy, yet the number of galaxies in the universe outnumbers the individual stars in our galaxy. Awe increases with knowledge!

When will we discern that all truth is God's truth? Only if our faith is in something or someone other than the God of our Lord Jesus Christ need we fear the truth. To believe that the God of Jesus Christ is both creator and redeemer is to believe that all truth is within God's creative and sustaining providence. Anything else in the place of God—even the Bible, the church, or religious principles and laws—can become an obstacle to faith in the one, living Lord of history.

134

Learning by its very nature will test the old with the new and vice versa. As one prayer has put it, which I have used in corporate worship, "Grant us patience to master the facts, candor to face the issues, wisdom to accept the mysteries, loyalty to truths already known, and courage to welcome new truth yet to be made known. In our task of learning, may we glorify Thee." Sometimes we forget that *everything* we now know, accept, and believe was absolutely brand-new the first time we considered or experienced it. Without accumulating an incredibly vast composite of new thoughts, facts, and experiences over many years, we could not have participated in any kind of process of becoming.

One of the most exciting trends in the 1970s was the explosion of adult learning and the revitalizing of our notions about adult life cycles. All kinds of "oldsters" defied ageism and returned to school for personal and professional purposes. In the past few years the Summer Conference Course of Study School held on the Saint Paul campus has enrolled students from their twenties to the upper seventies. As the average age of church members increases—and it seems to be doing just that—the concept of the body of Christ as a learning community becomes increasingly significant. While there is an always present fear of learning, there is also planted in the human heart and mind a thirst and hunger for learning. It is the church's task to turn this questing spirit into the joy of learning. And the joy of learning into the hallowing of life.

Directions, Dreams, and Designs for a Learned Laity

The Three Intersecting Circles upon which we reflected in chapter 3 are germane for laity learning as well as for clergy formation. It is a model that calls for attention to the life of the spirit, content, and methods, or as I suggested in the ordained ministry section, being, knowing, and doing. The church has more resources available than we realize for lifting up the learning church in all three of these areas.

In *Good News Is Bad News Is Good News,* as well as in the preceding chapter, I have suggested how liturgy can be a teaching instrument and a learning experience for the Body of Christ.[3] Liturgy as the work of the people provides a script or story out of which Christian life is lived in the world, a lay catechism or school of theology if you will. In that same work I pointed out how human relationships constitute a learning-source and a means of grace. In this chapter, however, I'm thinking primarily of the learning that can take place through intentionally designed efforts for adult growth or formation in a structured manner.

A beginning place is in our theological seminaries. If we hope to build a framework of expectation toward lay learning, we will begin by taking seriously the mutual ministry of laity and clergy and especially the function of clergy leadership as enablers and equippers of the laity. Unless this notion is taken seriously by clergy, ordination becomes the promotion of an elitist caste system instead of a community of servants.

It is my contention that every seminary student who is preparing for the ordained ministry should be ready upon graduation to teach at least one well-designed course for adults. High on my priority list would be a six- to eight-week course in one of the Gospels or in Romans. The biblical illiteracy of the church as a whole is appalling and constitutes one of the major contradictions to faithful and effective Christian ministry. *In the church we should be as concerned about biblical illiteracy as public educators are about illiteracy in terms of basic language and reading skills.*

In a devotional sense I believe that God can and does speak through the Bible to the person of faith apart from formal study of the Bible. A receiving, open attitude is a conduit for God's Word in Jesus Christ to come alive through the written Word, the Bible. But if we are to use the Bible as our primary source of direction and decision-making for the life and mission of the church in a complex world, a considerable amount of hard work and diligent study is required to allow the total text to speak the Word of God to us. Even then our own predispositions and prejudices may get in the way of a faithful hearing but at least the Bible will more likely have a chance to speak without distortion or bias.

I'll regret saying this, but to be candid about it, many laypersons are no more equipped to make biblically based decisions about the mission of the church in today's complexities than I am to fill a medical prescription from a pharmaceutical laboratory. Unless serious time and effort are given to the biblical texts and their original context, a person cannot make informed interpretations of their meaning for today's society. And of course even the most sophisticated biblical scholarship is no *guarantee* of responsible decision-making.

For the past several years I have been privileged to teach an intensive one-week course for seminary students called "The Practice of Parish Ministry." Using a variety of materials and educational methods, we work with a number of functions and issues of parish ministry. One of these is "The Pastor as Teaching Elder." Each student is asked to design an adult course of four-to-eight weeks which he/she proposes to teach in a congregation. Granted that any course will need to be shaped according to the particular context of the parish, the student is asked to deal with questions such as these: How and why was this particular subject or content chosen? What do you seek to accomplish, or what do you hope will happen as a result of the course? What methods will be used and why? What philosophy of learning informs your planning and methodology? What kind of setting do you foresee, such as physical environment, and age and background of participants? What kind of expectations will there be of the participants and how is this to be negotiated? What means of evaluation will be used at the

137

conclusion of the course? How will this course encourage care and mutual support of one another as well as new knowledge and insight? What part will the laity have in asking and answering these questions?

After each student is given planning and design time, small groups then convene to serve as supportive interaction units. Each design is further shared and reshaped according to the constructive questions and sharing of the group. Then we come together in a plenary session with several designs placed on the board for further analysis and reflection. The process itself is one of mutuality and cooperation rather than competition. In some cases the courses have *already* been taught and are reviewed for improvement.

My basic presupposition in dreaming for adult education designs is to strengthen the local, ongoing potential of the teaching ministry in the local church. Here you have relationship, convenience of location, and the advantage of ongoing conversation. A combination of a committed teacher who shares his or her faith and the presence of a caring community can go a long way in encouraging adult participation. Pastors who do not feel equipped to teach in the local church should track down the continuing education opportunities that offer training for a teaching ministry.

A design for major progress toward a learning church, however, will need to include the dimension of expectation and encouragement from church leaders, be they bishops, superintendents, or other denominational officials. It is increasingly expected that ordained ministers will be a learning example or model for the general church. Similarly lay leaders who assume key responsibilities for a year or more should be expected to commit themselves to a structured learning process. They should see themselves and be seen by others in the church as *accountable for serious adult formation in biblical literacy as a minimum, and hopefully in church history, a theology of worship, and the mission of the church.* Lay leaders would be regarded by their congregations and by the church-at-large as *accountable to the governing body of the congregation and to the ecclesiastical structure to which the ordained minister is immediately accountable.* To create and develop an ethos of expectations will take years and will need constant building up and renewing, just as with the continuing education of ordained ministers.

We now have expectations for the ordained that were almost unheard of a number of years ago, and we have moved toward far-reaching changes in the church unheard of only a couple of decades ago. For instance who would have dreamed in the 1950s—and perhaps even in the 1960s—that more than 20 percent of theological students in many seminaries would be women, most of whom are training for ordained ministry? Who would have foreseen the far-reaching changes in at least a significant minority of the Roman Catholic Church in South and Latin America who are clearly on the side of the poor and the oppressed?

I can imagine clergy and lay leaders within an area initiating a design for adult formation in the areas of biblical, historical, liturgical, and ethical literacy. The design would include an invitation to a leadership covenant by which leaders among the general ministry would make commitments as part of their acceptance of leadership, something like the commitments made in becoming church members. This design-invitation would be carefully processed in the appropriate structures in order to achieve maximum consultation and mutuality in the final results. The invitation of a system-wide approach would combine grass roots input with encouragement and expectation from denominational leadership.

Some pastors will say, "I have a hard enough time now securing leadership. What will it be like if we expect this kind of serious commitment?" What it will be like will be some new excitement and a deeper level of discipleship and mutual struggle. An area or judicatory will need to define all the available resources and arrange timing and geographical scheduling. Who are the pastors in this area of the state or in that district, presbytery, or diocese who are capable of teaching New Testament, church history, or ethics? Who are those having the ability to become trained to do so? Where are the nearest seminaries and/or other educational sources from which we can draw leadership in teaching?

In the 1970s the Nebraska Area of The United Methodist Church established in each district a Lay Theology Academy utilizing seminary professors from several schools. Courses were taught in key areas of theology, church history, and lay leadership. Considerable efforts were given to recruitment and participation. This was a move in the right direction. I can also imagine schools for lay leaders, just as we have Pastors' Schools in various denominations. For years the women of the church frequently have paved the way in adult formation through a wide assortment of educational courses. I do not mean to give the impression that nothing is going on now in adult formation. I am calling, however, for constructing a scaffolding for a more *comprehensive* and *intentional* ministry of teaching and learning, taking into consideration the complexities of lay schedules.

Another dream that I believe is within our reach is the concept of mutual learning for ordained and general ministers simultaneously. This book is one effort in that direction. How seldom it is that we sit *together* in the same classroom or series and learn together. Do we assume that the clergy is so far ahead of the laity that we cannot learn in common? Even though seminary-trained clergy have a head start in formal theological training, it seems to me that laity and clergy could be co-learners and that the clergy's training could help them assist the laity in their learning process. And how much the clergy can learn from laypersons who serve the church in the public areas of life! James C. Fenhagen holds before us similar visions for the church, providing as it turns out almost a summary of that which has been urged in this chapter. He lists these as signs of a shared ministry:

The realization that to be on a pilgrimage is of greater value than having all the answers. In this context clergy and laity are fellow pilgrims.

A system of accountability where both the ordained and lay leadership of the congregation are given feedback on the quality of the work they do.

Opportunities for the clergy to learn from the laity (where the laity set the agenda) at sufficient depth so as to be able to offer support in the exercise of their ministries outside the institutional church as well as opportunities for the laity to hear from the clergy in depth about their fears, needs, and concerns so as to offer support for their ministries.

Carefully designed and seriously perceived programs of lay theological education which are aimed at enabling laity to reflect on and interpret their daily experiences in light of what it means to be laos in the world.[4]

We need at least as "high" a view of the general ministers of the church as we do of the ordained ministers. The first disciples were a learning church. Today's faith seekers are accountable *to* God and the church *for* an intentional learning in the service of the world.

For Reflection and Discussion

1. What are the most important insights and values that you have learned in the Body of Christ?
2. What structured learning opportunities are available to you in the church and how can you envision a strengthening of these possibilities?
3. Does a theology of accountability for lay leaders have a place in the church? How do you see this taking place, either in actuality or in dreaming for the future?

Chapter 8

THE LOVING CHURCH

If you were going about the task of being the messiah and had three years, what would you do? If we had not already been influenced by the New Testament, our impulse might be to seek an audience with the most influential people in our world. Impact the centers of power. Convert those whose decisions could shape the future of civilization. The politicians rule the world, don't they? Washington. Moscow. Johannesburg. Peking. Paris. They can mobilize people and programs, even the use of nuclear force. But someone will say, "It's not the politicians who have the most power. It's the economists who call the shots. Forget the politicians. Show us the inflation index and the economic outlook!"

But then someone will assert that the real control of destiny resides with the military. A snap of the fingers and thousands perish or live. Economists included. A change of heart, then, in military heads. Yet still someone else is sure to claim that the future of the universe is in the hands of the scientists. Genetic codes and power to clone God knows what are in their hands. So as messiah-to-be, where will you begin?

The simplicity of the gospel narratives is overwhelming. One fact stands out in bold relief: *Jesus Christ, friend of sinners, sufferers, and Samaritans.* Bartimaeus. Peter. The Samaritan woman. Ten lepers. A man born blind. Lazarus. Mary. Martha. Matthew. Andrew. Zacchaeus. Peter's mother-in-law. The Gerasene demoniac. The hemorrhaging woman. Their names are legion. No "brightest and best" in this group. No power brokers and no names that graced the local social register or Herod's palace advisers.

Jesus is constantly moving toward those from whom others are moving away. Hardly a promising strategy to revolutionize the world! Love through preaching the rule of God; teaching the disciples and sometimes the multitudes; and healing and casting out demons. A love so radical that it cut through every legalism of organized religion. A love so grounded in the unmerited love of God for all people that some chose to crucify him while others chose to commit body and soul to him. A love so bound to the truth of God's reign that every power and principality would come under its dominion for better or worse—including politicians, economists, military leaders, and scientists. Jesus' messiahship was not disinterested in the great centers of world power. Quite the contrary. In his brief time he became the Incarnation of a truth that forever judges all systems of power, a truth calling for human dignity and justice.

Whatever else the church is called to be, nothing is more central than to become a loving community of Jesus Christ. In this chapter I will focus on love for individuals through the life of the church by using the concept of *care* as a basic expression of love. I do this in the hope of clarifying at least one dimension of what it means to love, a much maligned yet indispensable word to the people of God in ministry. Since God's loving care applies to systems and structures as well as individuals, chapter 9 will be concerned with the church's responsibility toward powers and principalities.

Actually the terms "love" and "liberation" both apply to individuals and to society, to spiritual and physical well-being. For purpose of reflection, however, I am choosing to utilize the concept of love in this chapter as it relates to caring for individuals, and the concept of liberation in the next chapter to point toward social caring and action.

THE PEOPLE OF GOD IN MINISTRY

Care as the Essence of All Ministries

Caring is the glue of all Christian ministry, whether lay or clerical. Where there is no caring, there is no Christian presence or action. We would not be in the community of Easter People had we not experienced care from others—a care that has made it possible for us to be caring toward others. Care is God's gift through Jesus Christ and the whole biblical tradition to be shared, not a virtue to be acquired. We love and care because we have first been loved and cared about by God through Jesus Christ and because that truth has been passed on to us by human hands and hearts within the Christian community.

For more than a decade I have found Peter Berger's description of Christian social engagement to be informative and useful. His categories suggest ways in which Christian caring takes place. In partially paraphrased form it looks like this:

1. *Christian diaconate*—the helping outreach of the Christian community to individuals in distress, such a those suffering from illness, poverty, or personal crisis. This emphasizes the primary importance of unspectacular and unpretentious Christian concern for the unique individual in his or her unique needs.

2. *Christian action*—the attempt of the church to modify or change the social system or structure itself. This action tries to induce social amendment in some direction thought desirable from the viewpoint of Christian ethics, and thus is aimed at cause as well as effect.

3. *Christian presence*—the erection of Christian signs in the world, such as identification with suffering where other recourses of social change are not possible, as in a suppressive state. An example would be voluntarily living among the poor and sharing their suffering where no other recourse is available.

4. *Christian dialogue*—the attempt to engage the world in conversation with the Christian faith in order to function as a

facilitator of communication between parties in complex ethical situations.[1]

Christian diaconate, as Berger defines it, is the primary method of Christian outreach through the Christian community, both within the membership of the church and beyond it. The practice of caring for others is "the daily currency" of the people of God in ministry and is a gift of God to be celebrated. All Christians can share the gifts of caring. When we look back on our experiences in the church through the years, the most vivid and memorable occasions will have to do with caring. I believe this is true for both laity and clergy.

In his excellent book, *Making the Small Church Effective*, Carl S. Dudley shares a wealth of research and experience. "In the small church, many pastors suggest two kinds of problems: they have overrated their power in changing the community and underrated their importance in touching the lives of people." He goes on to say, "I believe that a church is as large as the lives that are touched through the congregation, by the love of God. Caring is the ultimate measure of a congregation's size."[2]

While the small church may be less impressive than others in budgets, buildings, or bodies (as Dudley puts it), it is often well equipped for personal caring and responding to persons in personal need. This care about people is expressed in individual acts of kindness, food pantries, upgrading of community services, and meeting the needs of child care and of senior citizens. This fabric of caring is basic to Christian witness and outreach.

When our family moved from Dallas to the Kansas City area in 1973, it represented a major "roots pulling" since we had experienced all of our family life in the Dallas area. A great deal of caring and being cared about over the years in two pastorates was processed in grief and celebrated at the same time. The parting words of one couple seemed to sum up a number of relationships and our feelings about our times together: "We'll remember two things above all else. You were the first pastor who ever visited our home. And you buried our baby." Ministry is caring and being cared about.

The great moments and memories of ministry have to do with caring—caring for others, helping others learn to express caring, and being cared about. From time to time I reflect on the people with whom I've been privileged to serve through the years. Many of them in my first two appointments seem to fit the description given by Thomas Merton in *The Seven Storey Mountain* as he remembers the people in a small French village during a time of his youth:

> It is a great pleasure for me to remember such good and kind people. . . . I just remember their kindness and goodness to me, and their peacefulness and their utter simplicity. They inspired real reverence, and I think, in a way, they were certainly saints. And they were saints in that most effective and telling way: sanctified by leading ordinary lives in a completely supernatural manner, sanctified by obscurity, by usual skills, by common tasks, by routine, but skills, tasks, routine which received a supernatural form from grace within, and from the habitual union of their souls with God in deep faith and charity.
>
> Their farm, their family, and their Church were all that occupied these good souls; and their lives were full.[3]

Did you notice in Berger's description of Christian diaconate mentioned a few paragraphs above that he refers to Christian concern for the unique individual as *unspectacular* and *unpretentious?* Seminarians take note! Practicing pastors take note! Most laypersons already know this by experience as well as in an intellectual sense. The faithful and ongoing caring offered by many laypersons from day to day is frequently an example from which pastors can learn. Like everything else profound in life, caring has its ups and downs, its times of exhilaration and discouragement. Care is often hard work, whether for individuals or for institutions.[4] But loving care is the name of it all. If that doesn't turn you on, neither ordained nor the general ministry (laity) of the church will touch you deeply.

THE LOVING CHURCH

Looking Inside Caring

On the cover of Milton Mayeroff's book *On Caring* there is a penetrating insight into the meaning of caring. "In the sense in which a man can ever be said to be at home in the world, he is at home not through dominating . . . but through caring and being cared for."[5] He goes on to describe how life attains a sense of integration through caring, that is, of "being in place" or at home. Certain studies have shown the grace and power of caring in that retired widows and widowers who have pets to care for are more likely to have better health since there is a relationship that calls for caring attention.

In a short seminary course, "The Practice of Parish Ministry," I ask participants to reflect on a profound or powerful experience of caring and being cared about that they would be willing to share with one another. As best we are able in our reflection, we are to get in touch with what made this an unusually moving occasion, what we learned about ourselves, and what we learned about the meaning of caring and being cared about. I would like here to lift up the recurring insights that have come from our sharing, as well as an unforgettable experience of caring in my own life.

Again and again participants mention the *undeserved* nature of the gift of being cared about. Often the impact is overpowering and unforgettable. Sheer gift! No paternalism. No strings attached. Not because we were deserving but because someone else chose to give us the incredible gift of loving care. In the classroom sharing of these experiences, we often find it difficult to explain in words. Somehow we are in touch with the power of God's love in Jesus Christ. When that becomes incarnate in a relational gift, we experience the deepest reality of existence. Our worth is reconfirmed in spite of all our hangups and our strategies to make ourselves acceptable as "somebody."

In November 1978, I had the opportunity to travel in Japan for about four days before proceeding to South Korea. Several

months before the trip I entered into correspondence with
Masashi Miura, a Tokyo resident whom I had never met but
whose name was given to me by a mutual friend. Our plans were
set. After arrival in Narita Airport on Japan Airlines, I was to
catch the airport bus to the downtown City Air Terminal where
Masashi would meet me according to precise instructions he had
sent.

Unfortunately I had an incomplete visa in my passport due to
an administrative foul-up in the United States. After endless
discussions with the immigration officials at Narita Airport, I
was given the choice of appealing to the Minister of Justice for
approval of a correct visa or else restricting my stay to
seventy-two hours in Tokyo. Since one of my major objectives
for travel in Japan was a two-day excursion to Kyoto, I chose the
appeal. If it were to fail, they would ship me out of the country
on the next plane following rejection.

I was quarantined in the Narita Airport Hotel pending the
decision. Lest I give the wrong impression, I need to make clear
that the hotel was not exactly like a prison; in fact, precisely the
opposite—much more expensive than desirable! Fortunately, I
was able to contact Masashi through the immigration officials.
He volunteered to come to the hotel the next morning and sit
with me during the waiting period and in addition to use any
influence that he might have in the process. I cannot remember
ever being so grateful to meet a stranger and to have his
company!

After about seven hours in my hotel room, following several
false alarms, we received word that my appeal had been
approved. I could stay! During the next two days Masashi
showered me with an unbelievable generosity and hospitality in
between his own teaching responsibilities at Takoshoku
University. Took me to my hotel in Tokyo following my
"release." Provided instructions to make connections with a
morning tour of Tokyo the next day. Went with me on the
intricate subway system to the Meiji Shrine. Introduced me to

his family and graciously had me as his dinner guest, an experience I'll never forget. Took me back to the hotel. Provided transportation to the train station, having obtained the correct ticket for my trip on the bullet train (Shinkansen) to Kyoto. Spoke with the Japanese men with whom I was seated on the train and asked them to take care of me and to point out Mt. Fuji. Waited outside the coach until the train departed. I had not been so deeply moved in a long, long time.

The two days in Kyoto were marvelous. Then it was time to return to Tokyo. It was at that moment that I realized anew the remarkable power and beauty of caring. What a difference *one person in twelve million* made, even a person I had met only four days before! Why, Tokyo was my "home away from home," because I knew Masashi and I was known and cared for by him! I returned on the train to Tokyo. I went out to dinner, explored the Ginza shopping area, went to the Kabuki Theater, and returned to my hotel room. The next day Masashi was to pick me up at 6:00 A.M. to take me to the Downtown City Air Terminal to begin my trip to Korea. Before retiring for the evening I had a telephone call from the hotel lobby. Wouldn't you know it? Masashi, bearing gifts for me, my wife, and my children!

Never in my life will I forget this amazing grace-filled experience. I learned that relationships and the care they provide can easily be taken for granted because I am accustomed to familiar faces and places. When I travel in the United States, it is nearly always to a conference or to a meeting where I am known and know others. On the Japan-Korea trip I knew that I most likely would not see a single face among thousands that I had ever seen before. But I was not prepared for the overpowering and empowering grace of one person's care for me, a care that I had done absolutely nothing to deserve.

Another recurring theme in the class's sharing of caring experiences, closely related to the first, is our *difficulty in receiving.* We are so programmed by our society into justifying ourselves and protecting ourselves that we can barely stand to receive a gift. Or is it that a deep sense of unworthiness blocks our capacity to receive? Ordained ministers, imagining ourselves as capable givers, sometimes have special difficulty in receiving the gifts of others. One of my most important discoveries in the pastorate came to me some years ago during a bout with mononucleosis, combined with a violent reaction to penicillin. The outpouring of care nourished me as a person during the seven-week period of convalescence and helped release me from needing to be "in control" of the congregation's activities.

A third realization from our class sharing was *how much* even a little care can mean to people who have run out of people to touch and be touched by. We never really know when and in what ways that may be true for anyone at a given time. I recall an occasion of eating in a restaurant with a friend when he paid a very simple compliment to a teen-age employee. My friend had used the men's room and found it sparkling clean. Then as we were downing our hamburger, we noticed a teen-age employee who was cleaning tables. My friend asked him if he were responsible for cleaning the men's rest room. Apprehension appeared on the teen-ager's face as he replied in the affirmative. My friend proceeded to express appreciation for a job well done. By the smile and uplift immediately visible, you would have thought it was the first compliment ever received by the teen-ager for his work. The sad truth is that it may have been.

The most exciting meaning in caring happens when the recipient is thereby moved to care about someone else as a consequence of being cared about.

Caring as an Expression of Love

Jesus is not recorded in the Revised Standard Version of the New Testament as having used the word "care" except in the good Samaritan story. The most important ingredients of care are reflected in the care provided by the Samaritan and in his request to the innkeeper to do likewise at the Samaritan's expense. Time. Risk. Patience. Humility. Courage. Hope. The reward for caring is of course the act of caring itself. There is no guarantee that our care will bring about some kind of visible result, either in or for the person cared about or in his or her attitude toward us. Nor is the act of caring dependent, in a Christian sense, on our opinion of the one in need.

Victor Paul Furnish touches on this point and helps us see caring in relation to the New Testament love command in these statements:

> The love Jesus commanded, be it directed toward the "neighbor" or toward the "enemy," is understood in just one way: as active goodwill toward the other, as my affirmation of him as a person who stands or falls quite apart from what I think of him, as my acknowledgment of our common humanity and our common dependence upon One whose judgment and mercy is over all, and as my commitment to serve him in his need.
>
> In Paul . . . (love) means *caring* for the other—not because of who he is or where he stands in relation to oneself, but just because he *is*, and because he is *there*. It means *identifying* with him, with his needs, his hurts, his joys, his hopes, his lostness and loneliness. It means being willing to *risk taking the initiative in reconciliation*, and being willing, finally, to *give oneself* to him in service and support for his humanity. In Christ one is a recipient of such love and thereby becomes a participant in the new creation. By love he is freed—to love; for love is the meaning of his obedience and his life.[6]

Easter People are called to be lovers and carers above all else because we have received a largess of unconditional love. Usually caring is anonymous in the sense that it is unpretentious and unspectacular. Occasionally it is dramatic, as in the following story told to me by a layman in Nebraska:

A member of the governing board of a certain congregation

was indicted and convicted of embezzlement in a financial institution where he was employed. He was sentenced to several months in a correctional institution some fifty miles away. Every week—without fail—two members of the church's governing board made the trip to see their friend, visiting, offering encouragement, and learning what would be most helpful. At last when the time came for the man to be released, the entire governing board of the congregation met him at the entrance gate to embrace him and welcome him home again. *Jesus Christ, friend of sinners, sufferers, and Samaritans.* Need we debate the relevance of the Easter People when they *are!*

The ministry of caring is the calling of all Christians into the fright and loneliness of life. The Easter People are a "being with" people who remember an empty tomb and who look for intimations of resurrection in the dark hours. Henri J. Nouwen underscores a biblical understanding of care: "The gospel is not a palliative to help us escape the pain of life, but the way to transform suffering into the birth pangs of something new . . . ministry works through pain, taking *care* to be with people, to love them, to share their pain."[7]

The sense of lostness in our generation—the boredom, the narcissism, the lack of direction—could be revolutionized through simple acts of caring about others. We have it on good authority that those who lose their lives in care for others will find themselves anew in a most remarkable way. A friend told me recently that he felt a whole new wave of excitement about himself and about living. The occasion for this breakthrough was simply helping his neighbor dig a car out from entrapment in ice and snow. "I didn't realize," my friend said to me later, "that my whole life had become completely centered around myself. I hadn't done anything to help someone else for so long that I'd forgotten how wonderful it can be!" Caring can rejuvenate or rekindle our sense of self and a deeper sense of purpose in life.

The theme song of the people of God in ministry could well

152

be Paul Scherer's memorable insight into Christ-centered love: "Love is a spendthrift, never keeps score, and is always in the red."

Take some time now to meditate on great moments of caring, both giving and receiving, in your life. If you have been as fortunate in both as I, your remembrance will call back countless gifts and graces and many special people. Most of our "significant others" are either carers who have touched us in special ways and times, or those for whom we have cared deeply, or both.

On the Move from Head to Toes

What are the qualifications of a good pastor? Try this: Must have small family, if any, and be able to furnish a house and come to church unassisted. Must not be afraid to work, have a good clear head, a warm, loving heart—and big feet. An advertisement in the Methodist Recorder of Pittsburgh, September 17, 1903.

Not a bad definition of Easter People, both clergy and laity. People with "big feet," moving toward those in need. *Jesus Christ, friend of sinners, sufferers, and Samaritans.*

For Reflection and Discussion

1. In what ways do you as a church member give and receive care in your congregation?
2. How does your congregation express care to persons beyond the congregation? How do you take seriously Jesus Christ, Friend of sinners, sufferers, and Samaritans?
3. What is done in your congregation to strengthen and deepen the ministry of lay pastoral care?

Chapter 9

THE LIBERATING CHURCH

"Let's get back to the Bible!" This exhortation, frequently heard in the church, can have different meanings. It could suggest that we cease to water down God's Word with the use of pop psychology. Or the exhorter could be urging the church to appreciate its charter and written foundation. It could mean that we tell it like it is or that we need to major in grace, with less emphasis on moralistic and legalistic approaches. But in my experience it has usually been an insistence on separating faith from involvement in some dimension of life.

The truth is that we *never have* and *never will* "get back to the Bible" because the Bible is always out in front of us beckoning us to catch up with its vision of life. The resurrection narratives all suggest that those who sought Jesus expected to find him in a predictable location in yesterday's experience, namely, the tomb. Instead, the seekers at early dawn found that the risen Lord had already preceded them and had gone *before* them to Galilee (Matt. 28:6-7 and Mark 16:6-7). The risen Lord will not be bound!

The Easter experience is a catch-up experience. The Suffering One is the Sovereign One who has preceded us not only through creation but also in re-creation. The Risen One has always gone before us. On the road to Emmaus. In the breaking of bread. In daily occupation. In the command to love him by loving those in need. To be sure, the risen Christ is the Jesus who taught and healed and loved in the past. Yet he will not be limited to either memory or past experience. No wonder the response of the seekers is one of trembling, amazement, and joy. If we cannot deposit him securely in the past, where will he lead us in the future? To become an Easter People is to play catch-up to the risen, on-the-move Lord of life and history.

We have never gotten back to the Bible, because we have never caught up with its call to shalom and reconciliation. When have we ever beat our swords into plowshares and our spears into pruning hooks? When have we as a human race done justice and walked humbly with our God? When has the church through the masses of its people spoken clearly on behalf of human rights, equality, and dignity for all?

What does it mean for the church to catch up with our risen Lord? What would it look like for the church to refuse to reduce faith into privatism, to boldly insist that God is God of *all* creation, that Jesus is Lord of *all* powers and principalities as well as personal piety? What if the church regarded religion as inseparable from life itself, like the Zuni Indians for whom this inseparability is reflected in the lack of an equivalent for the English word "religious"? In this chapter let's explore some contours of a church willing to follow the risen Lord into every hunger, every thirst, every form of suffering and deprivation, every form of imprisonment (Matt. 25:31-46).

The Easter Issue: God's Whereabouts

The church by and large has always had a blind spot when it comes to Easter interpretation. Contrary to the explicit narratives in the Gospels, we have tended to center our attention *only* on the assurance of God's eternal providence and care for us. Certainly Paul places a strong emphasis on God's everlasting and all-embracing love. Indeed, through the years one of my favorite texts for my funeral messages has been exactly this affirmation from Romans 14:7-9: "None of us lives to himself, and none of us dies to himself. If we live, we live to the Lord; so then, whether we live or whether we die, we are the Lord's. For to this end Christ died and lived again, that he might be Lord both of the dead and of the living." Paul is proclaiming a God who is Lord of all creation, both life and death. We are forever embraced in God's presence, being raised up even in death into God's eternity. Faith does not need to know the whys, hows, and wherefores of God's love. Faith already trusts in the unlimited whereabouts of God's presence and love.

There is, in addition, a second sense in which the Easter story proclaims the presence or whereabouts of God. This second sense is not absent in Paul's writing, but it becomes *primary* in the Gospel accounts. It has always struck me as peculiar that the church has not made more of God's whereabouts in the Easter narratives of the Gospels. For in these stories the clear and unambiguous emphasis of the risen Lord is not in life beyond this world but in *mission here and now*. One only has to read the narratives themselves to confirm their concentration on ministry to the present age. It matters not whether the narratives have been faithfully preserved in the period of oral transmission or whether they represent evangelistic additions by the early church or combinations of both.

In Matthew's account, the risen Lord announces that all authority in heaven and earth has been given to him. He then gives the great commission, "Go therefore and make disciples of all nations, baptizing them in the name of the Father and of the Son and of the Holy Spirit, teaching them to observe all that I have commanded you; and lo, I am with you always, to the close of the age" (Matt. 28:19-20). In the standard Markan text those who come to the tomb are told that Jesus has risen and is going before them into Galilee. There are no conversations between Jesus and his followers, nor are there any words of Jesus.

Luke pictures the risen Jesus in very physical ways participating in ordinary events of the disciples' experience (Luke 24). He hallows the journey on the road and the everyday experience of breaking bread and being together. In other words he appears in the very *structures* of their daily lives. He assures his followers that it is he who is present and that he is truly present.

He instructs his followers to preach repentance and the forgiveness of sins in his name to all nations. Their joy following his departure appears to be due to the assurance that the risen Lord will be with them as they carry out the tasks that he has given them to do.

In John 20 the risen Jesus appears to Mary and then to the disciples. Jesus says to them, "Peace be with you. As the father has sent me, even so I send you" (v. 21). Then he confers upon them the Holy Spirit, as though to be with them as they are sent. In chapter 21 a failure in fishing is turned into an abundant catch. Then fish and bread are shared. Then the famous story in which Simon Peter is asked thrice by Jesus, "Do you love me?" Each time Peter's verbal assurance is countered with, "Feed my lambs. Tend my sheep. Feed my sheep." This passage appears to be related in meaning to Matthew's parable of the last judgment (Matt. 25:31-46). What's on Jesus' mind, both before and after the resurrection, is Christian witness in the crucible of a needy world.

Thus, Easter is a proclamation of the risen Lord in every pocket of need, in every nook and cranny of creation. God's whereabouts are not limited to our preferences or choices. For those who wish to restrict religion to personal piety or to a special segment of creation, Easter is *bad* news! God is not dead, Easter tells us. God's whereabouts are inscribed across the terrain of all life. For this reason the religion of the Easter People knows no limits or departments because the whereabouts of the risen Lord knows no limits.

Easter and the Liberating Church

In chapter 8 I indicated that I would be focusing on "The Loving Church" as it related to loving care for individuals. Also I noted that in chapter 9 I would invite you to reflect with me on the relationships of Easter People to structures and systems of our society and world. Although I am using the liberating church as a lens through which to look at powers and principalities, I again want to affirm that love and liberation in actuality are both concerned with the personal and the social. God's largess to Easter People calls forth the ministry of all Christians to all of life and history. To settle for less is to openly acknowledge that God is either unconcerned or dead in the great arenas of decision-making and influence that impact life and history. With this back-to-the-Bible stance in mind, consider with me four marks of a liberating church.

1. *Easter faith has to do with politics and economics as much as prayer and piety.*

One of the great tragedies of Christian history is the confusion between separation of church and state on the one hand, and the absence of moral and human concerns from economics and politics on the other. Theologically, evil is sometimes understood to be the absence of the good. Nothing contributes more to inhumane and oppressive systems in our world than for "the good" to be silent and do nothing.

History is rife with examples of political and economic oppression. The enslavement of the Hebrews under Pharaoh is an excellent example and is a critical reminder that getting back to the Bible, so to speak, is getting back to the involvement of God in the political and economic realm. If Pharaoh had been interviewed during the confrontation with Moses, he would have said that Moses should stick to religion and stay out of politics. Members of Pharaoh's religion might have seen Moses as an "outsider" who didn't know the facts and who had no business meddling in "secular" matters. But the God of Exodus and Easter is an "everywhere" God who meddles in all oppressive systems in order to liberate the oppressors from their bondage to sin and the oppressed from a dehumanizing and degrading enslavement. The God of history makes no distinction between secular and sacred. There is one life, one history, and one Lord.

THE LIBERATING CHURCH

When Hitler came to power in Germany in the early 1930s, he told a gathering of pastors in Berlin that they could take care of their parishioners' souls and that he would take care of politics and economics. This arrangement has been repeated by virtually every oppressive government in history, whether leftist or rightist. The Easter People should see political and economic issues not as areas divorced from faith or religion, but as *moral, ethical,* and *human* matters under the sovereignty of God. Separation of church and state, or church and economics, or church and anything else, rightfully protects against church control of systems for which we do not have the required expertise. It is not our task or calling to design and operate political or economic systems. It *is* our calling to raise the moral question, to condemn oppression, and to call for amendment of systems that degrade human life. To separate moral and ethical imperatives from *any* area of life is a disaster for life and a betrayal of the church's mission of love and liberation.

To get back to the Bible, or as I have suggested, to catch up with the Bible, is to have an acute awareness of the sovereignty of God over *all* powers and principalities. I have long advocated a mandatory course in Isaiah, with special emphasis on the fortieth chapter, for all public servants in the United States. While I am being a bit facetious, not by much! Any Christian who reads this magnificent panoramic view of God's sovereignty over history cannot restrict God to our personal prayers as important as they are. Our failure to recognize God as the Everywhere One is a failure to take the Bible seriously and a failure to receive the Good News of Easter.

Easter and Christmas confirm each other since the Incarnation also was witness to the Everywhere God. The Incarnation has overcome the spirit-matter dualism that characterized a good deal of ancient thought as well as that of present-day Christians. Bonhoeffer claimed that only Christians who spoke out for the Jews in the 1930s and 1940s could sing Gregorian chants with authenticity. It is also the case in my opinion that only Christians who clearly affirm the rights of women and the dignity and equality of ethnic persons are entitled to sing Easter and Christmas hymns!

Today's issues are so many and complex that it is all too easy to plead either ignorance or helplessness. Each Christian who can do so would do well to make an effort to become well informed on at least one major issue; examine your life and change your life according to where the Spirit of Christ is leading you in relation to that issue; and become an advocate who helps educate others. What will be your choice: peace; environment; the rights and needs of children or of aging persons; justice for ethnic minorities; support of women in ministry, as persons, and as citizens; human rights across the world; concern about violence in our society?

Liberation from oppression is a central theme throughout the Old Testament, with particular focus in the Exodus Event and in the message of Amos, Isaiah, and other prophets.[1] Isaiah's clarion call to justice and message of good tidings to the afflicted (Isa. 61) become the core of Jesus' ministry according to Luke (4:18-19) and the text for his sermon in the synagogue at Nazareth. A liberating church will come back again and again to this text:

> The Spirit of the Lord is upon me, because he has anointed me to preach good news to the poor. He has sent me to proclaim release to the captives and recovering of sight to the blind, to set at liberty those who are oppressed, to proclaim the acceptable year of the Lord. (Luke 4:18-19)

2. *Easter faith embraces the gifts and graces of God for the whole person—spirit, soul, intellect, emotions, body.*

All through the Gospels Jesus is ministering to the whole person. The Incarnation fuses together spirit and matter, soul and body, word and flesh. So did Easter. Jesus appeared in the most ordinary and *real* experiences of life. Eating. Meeting.

Journeying. Working. Thus Christian theology does not have to choose up sides between saving souls and saving people from starvation, or between spiritual and material bread.

It is a judgment on the church that today's theologies emphasizing release from poverty, marginal existence, and dehumanization are considered by some to be peripheral or even faddish. The story of the good Samaritan, who took seriously the physical needs of another human, is hardly a fad. Neither is the parable of the last judgment. Biblical theology is by its very nature a *liberation theology* opposing injustice related to race, sex, age, or economic class. A liberating church is one committed to working *for* a community of justice and dignity for all.

Few Christians have more faithfully brought together vital piety and social caring than John Wesley. Lest this sound like Methodist "triumphalism," it had best be said that our history gives us no excuse to disparage either soul or body. No one could be more passionate than Wesley in the saving of souls or at least in understanding his calling as God's instrument of soul saving. But then no one could be more passionate in social involvement either. Was there any significant social ill in which Wesley did not meddle, as his adversaries would have put it?

3. Easter faith is as concerned about causes as about symptoms.

It has often been said that individual charity is regarded as a saintly deed whereas the same concern focused on a change of systems can lead to martyrdom! Many Christians give assent to the use of moral persuasion as a means of bringing about needed change. But the use of power or nonviolent legal means is often depreciated. The problem of course is that entrenched power almost never responds to moral persuasion. In seeking to change causes as well as ministering to symptoms one quickly learns some hard facts about how the world is put together.

When I was a pastor of a new congregation on the east side of Dallas (Mesquite) in the early 1960s, the difference between the church as charity-giver and as change-bringer came to the forefront. A Presbyterian pastor shared with me his concern for a number of black families who lived near his parish area. The children of these families attended a three-room schoolhouse that was crammed with eight grades. There were no sidewalks. No playground equipment. Not even a flagpole. The senior high students were shipped by bus to a segregated school in another community some forty miles down the highway. In the meantime, the local school system had just completed a brand new high school with first class facilities.

To tell you the truth I had been busy with my own congregation for the most part. New members. Building plans. Committees. Sermons. Newsletters. Visitations. But I couldn't get those black children and youth out of my mind. So the Presbyterian pastor and I visited the families. Poor. Scared. Uncertain. Invisible in the community.

They told us they would support us, the two pastors, in taking the initiative in approaching the school board. We worked out a mutually agreed strategy, realizing as fully as we could the possible risks. I shared the issue and the plan with my lay leaders in the congregation. We discussed possible reactions from members should it come to that. The leadership of the congregation was supportive.

The next meeting of the school board included two pastors and two laypersons on the agenda. We had decided that lay representation from each congregation would be representative and also strengthen our case. The black families were very vulnerable, and while strongly backing our appearance before the school board, chose not to be visibly involved at this point. We made our presentation, explaining our concerns and urging through moral persuasion that an unjust situation be remedied. Our style was gracious, the response polite. They would give it consideration.

Time went by. No response. No action. After a personal visit with the superintendent, it was clear that avoidance and evasion were the names of the game.

We went back to the planning stage. More conversation with the black families. More discussion in our church councils. Consensus: moral persuasion, appealing to goodwill and human decency, was of no avail. Just like Reinhold Niebuhr said it in *The Nature and Destiny of Man.* Some say seminary is an ivory tower and that the people know how it really is. Not in this case. Niebuhr had played all the cards in Detroit while a pastor. Many laypersons will counsel moral persuasion and that only! Or is it that they just don't want any trouble in spite of a crucified Lord? Next move! Legal persuasion. The only alternative is to give in to a blatant injustice. Which would you recommend?

Following a certain amount of runaround, we managed to get on the school board agenda for a second try. Again we reiterated the injustice and requested some sure sign of serious response. Anger from members of the school board. Our response: your policy and practice are not only immoral, but also in violation of the United States Constitution. Gentlemen (they *were* all male), we'll see you in court. Silence. Departure of the four visitors.

Within three days the school superintendent initiated contact with us and asked for a meeting. The school board, having imaged itself before the public as progressive and with a commitment to excellence, had voted to begin the next semester with an inclusive arrangement. A program would be established to insure as smooth a transition as possible for all concerned, including students and teachers of both races. As things turned out, the plan went into operation and an inclusive school system came into being.

Never before had the school board been confronted with Christians who meant business, who believed Jesus Christ to be present in the public as well as the private arena. If we had had to go to court, I don't know where we would have raised the necessary money. But we would have raised it. During the process we experienced an exodus of some members who didn't want "their church" to be "involved in politics." It hurt when they left, but it would have hurt more if we had been content to mind our own church business at the expense of social justice and a decent opportunity for some invisible folk in our community. After all, if God is willing to send plagues of blood, frogs, gnats, flies, hail, boils, and locusts to overcome Pharaoh's oppression, a few twentieth-century devotees ought to be able and willing to send a plague of law-suits to honor the tradition. I've always felt that in this encounter my faith took on a deeper meaning, that the church matched its creeds with its deeds.

I might not have had the required courage apart from the support of some very special lay members of the congregation who were possessed with an Easter faith. Ever since then my view of evangelism has been influenced by what occurred. Most of our members who departed our congregation became members of another Methodist church across the highway. From comments that drifted back by the grapevine, I got the impression that they never had to worry in their new church home about things like school systems, black families, social ills, or bad publicity. One church had lost some members. Another showed an increase on the rolls. To this day I am unable to make an unquestioned assumption about whether or not Christian evangelism has indeed taken place by merely looking at numerical growth on the membership rolls.

As I was writing this chapter an article appeared in *The Kansas City Times* describing the stockholders activity of the Sisters of Loretto. The Order buys shares of stock as a vehicle to register social protest through resolutions at stockholders' meetings. The aim is to bring about reform in blatant labor and environmental abuses. For example one company's 4,600 federal violations since 1970 had earned it one of the nation's worst mine safety records.

In today's context this affirmation of the God of justice is parallel to Wesley's protest against slavery in his times. If we as Easter People are serious about the causes of social injustices as well as the effects, we will need to be more committed, more sophisticated in strategy, and more willing to take risks than merely confronting powerful vested interests with polite verbal requests. Are we really serious about the Everywhere God or are we content to wash our hands?

When we address ourselves to basic causes as well as symptoms of human ills, we need to be prepared to work with complexity and ambiguity, and thus with the possibility of making mistakes. But mistakes in judgment from time to time seem more preferable to me than a faith that washes its hands of the world's injustices.

The basic tenets of the social gospel, subject as they are to sentimental optimism and utopian intellectualism, nevertheless retain a veracity for every generation. The vision of Walter Rauschenbusch, prophet of the social gospel in the early part of this century, is as valid today as it was in his time:

> The social gospel is the old message of salvation, but enlarged and intensified. The individualistic gospel has taught us to see the sinfulness of every human heart and has inspired us with faith in the willingness and power of God to save every soul that comes to him. But it has not given us an adequate understanding of the sinfulness of the social order and its share in the sins of all individuals within it. It has not evoked faith in the will and power of God to redeem the permanent institutions of human society from this inherited guilt of oppression and extortion. Both our sense of sin and our faith in salvation have fallen short of the realities under its teaching. The social gospel seeks to bring men under repentance for their collective sins and to create a more sensitive and more modern conscience. It calls on us for the faith of the old prophets who believed in the salvation of nations.[2]

4. *The Easter faith of a liberating church will lead us to identify with the suffering and deprivation of people around the world.*

A congregation has already lost part of its soul if it does not see itself as related to the global context of God's story. Whether through a Heifer Project or by petitions to government heads in support of human rights, Easter people belong at the crossroads of the world. Sometimes suffering is caused by defective systems and structures. But because the risen Lord appeared in the common experience and structures of our daily existence, it is our job as Christians to speak out and act out against oppressive systems where possible. All over the world in our generation, Christians are putting themselves on the line. Where are we?

A Clue for Coping with Controversy

Some things in life are predictable. One of them is at least occasional controversy in a congregation that takes seriously its call to be a liberating people. I never looked forward to controversy when I was a pastor. However, if there is to be controversy and acrimonious behavior, I would rather have it over great issues than over the roof leak in the sanctuary, the color of the carpet in the nursery, or the exact volume of the organ prelude. And as Robert K. Hudnut observed, better to have a divided church that stands for something than a united church that stands for nothing.

During the Vietnam War I took a position against our involvement, but only after a prodigious amount of homework and research. I preached two sermons on the issue, attempting to provide a biblical and theological foundation. Further, I was involved in the Dallas Chapter of Clergy and Laity Concerned About the Vietnam War. As one might expect, the response from the congregation was quite mixed. It became apparent that we needed an opportunity for members of the congregation to face one another, as well as the pastor, on the issue.

An evening was set aside for all viewpoints to be expressed. A panel of three held forth: a dove, a hawk, and an undecided. Much discussion followed. Reasonable but intense. When everyone had had their say, we formed a circle composed of about thirty-five to forty persons for a service of Holy

Communion. The associate pastor and I made some comments, consecrated the elements, and passed the loaf and the chalice to the persons next to us. Each person was free to drink from the common chalice or to use the intinction method, then passing the loaf and the chalice to the next person either in silence or with whatever words he or she deemed appropriate. As one member offered the elements to his neighbor with whom he was in strong disagreement about the war, he said, "Hang in there, Harvey." Not exactly the historic words of distribution, but nevertheless containing grace!

We participated in an unforgettable paschal mystery. All our individual conflicting beliefs had been expressed, yet we were caught up in one faith in the Crucified-Risen Lord. Our differences were sustained and accepted by the One in whom we live, and move, and have our being. In the victory of that One the Easter People can be whole, even in controversy.

The Church's Social Standing

The liberating church struggles with the question of its social standing. That standing needs to be examined again and again as we face the issues of hunger, human rights, racism, and sexism. Thus, Dorothee Sölle, who teaches on the faculty of Union Theological Seminary in New York, has equated "taking up your cross" with breaking neutrality and making it clear that you are on the side of the oppressed and marginal people. The basic decision is whether or not we will conform to a social standing as defined by society or be transformed by Easter faith into a social standing identified with *all* of those for whom Christ died.

For Reflection and Discussion

1. As you reflect on the life of the church today and in recent years, can you point to times when you were glad that the

church spoke out on public policy or became involved in a
social issue? And times when you either had serious
reservations or outright disagreement with such involvement?

2. As you get in touch with these events, how do you trace your
   response—whether positive or negative—to a biblical and
   theological orientation?

3. How does the congregation to which you belong reveal itself
   to be deeply concerned with some of the great issues of our
   time, such as peace, energy conservation, world hunger,
   racism, and sexism?

Postscript
THE LEAVENING CHURCH

At the entrance of Dante's hell there appear these words: "Abandon hope, all ye who enter here." Human history seems bent on crossing the point of no return on the way to Dante's hell. You already know the doomsday scenario, so I'll not belabor the point.

Listening. Learning. Loving. Liberating. In receiving and exemplifying these gifts of God, the Easter People become *a leaven of hope* for the future. Hope is a mode of discernment that goes beyond optimism and pessimism. For Christian hope has roots in the Suffering-Sovereign One of history, the Exodus-Easter God in whom we live and move and have our being.

In her book, *The Hiding Place,* Corrie ten Boom tells the harrowing tale of life in Ravensbrueck, a Nazi concentration camp for women during World War II. She relates how a few of the prisoners managed to conduct clandestine Bible study sessions in spite of everything. In referring to the barracks where the meetings were held, the other prisoners called it "the crazy place where they have hope." Not a bad definition of the Christian community—The Crazy People who have hope!

NOTES

Chapter 1

1. Even The United Methodist Church booklet for candidacy in ministry, *The Christian as Minister*, barely provides clues to the basic burdens and blessings for which the candidate is preparing.

2. For a study of the biblical character of the church's ministry, see James D. Smart, *The Rebirth of Ministry* (Philadelphia: The Westminster Press, 1960, paperback 1979).

3. *The Book of Worship for Church and Home* (Nashville: The Methodist Publishing House, 1964), p. 387.

4. From Jurgen Moltmann, quoted in William K. McElvaney, *Cerebrations on Coming Alive* (Nashville: Abingdon, 1973), p. 116.

5. Rex Brico, *Taize*, from conversations with Brother Robert Schutz (New York: William Collins Sons & Co., 1978), p. 206.

6. Pablo Casals, *Joys and Sorrows*. His own story as told to Albert E. Kahn (New York: Simon & Schuster, 1970), p. 105.

7. A quote from Martha Graham on a 1973 letter from the office of the dean, Meadow School of the Arts, Southern Methodist University.

8. Smart, *The Rebirth of Ministry*, p. 38.

9. Paul Waitman Hoon, *The Integrity of Worship* (Nashville: Abingdon, 1971), p. 23.

10. John Burkhart, quote from a printed address, "First Things First," June 3, 1974.

11. Harvey Cox, *The Seduction of the Spirit* (New York: Simon & Schuster, 1973), p. 44.

12. McElvaney, *Cerebrations on Coming Alive*, p. 39.

13. Fritz Henle, *Casals* (New York: American Photographic Book Publishing Co., Inc., 1975).

14. From "An Artist in America," quoted in *The Kansas City Times* editorial, January 21, 1975.

Chapter 2

1. Richard John Neuhaus, "Freedom for Ministry," *The Christian Century*, February 2-9, 1977, p. 86.

2. Harvey Cox, *The Seduction of the Spirit* (New York: Simon & Schuster, 1973). p. 44.

3. Bill Presnell, "The Minister's Own Marriage," *Pastoral Psychology,* Summer, 1977.

4. Harold A. Bosley, "The Minister as a Creative Critic," mimeographed paper, 1973. All quotes in the paragraph are from that paper.

5. Martin Luther, *A Commentary on St. Paul's Epistle to the Galatians.* Translated by Theodore Graebner, fourth edition. (Grand Rapids, Mich.: Zondervan Publishing House, n.d.), pp. 235, 242.

6. "Between Athens and Jerusalem: The Seminary in Tension," *The Christian Century,* February 4-11, 1976, pp. 90-92.

7. The writings of Joseph Campbell have contributed significantly to an understanding of religious stories and folktales. For example, the similarities of the basic truths are explored in *The Hero with a Thousand Faces,* first edition. (Princeton, N.J.: Princeton University Press, 1949).

Chapter 3

1. Excerpts from "Choruses from 'The Rock' " from COLLECTED POEMS 1909-1962 by T. S. Eliot, copyright, 1936, by Harcourt Brace Jovanovich, Inc.; copyright © 1963, 1964 by T. S. Eliot. Reprinted by permission of the publishers Harcourt Brace Jovanovich and Faber and Faber Ltd.

2. Thomas Merton, *The Seven Storey Mountain* (New York: Harcourt Brace Jovanovich, 1948), p. 3.

3. Gene E. Bartlett, *The Authentic Pastor* (Valley Forge, Pa.: Judson Press, 1978), p. 12.

4. Carl S. Dudley, *Making the Small Church Effective* (Nashville: Abingdon, 1978), pp. 71, 72.

5. William F. Lynch, S. J., *Images of Hope* (Notre Dame, Ind.: University of Notre Dame Press, 1965), p. 11.

Chapter 4

1. J. D. Salinger, *Franny and Zooey* (Boston: Little, Brown, 1955), pp. 147-48.

2. Hindu monasticism has a 5,000 year history: Buddhist monasticism approximately 2,000 years.

3. John T. McNeill, *The Celtic Churches,* (Chicago: University of Chicago Press, 1974).

4. David Knowles, *Christian Monasticism* (New York: McGraw-Hill Book Co., 1969).

5. While Friars of the Franciscan and Dominican orders had a role in the early development of the Spanish West, there were no *monks* in the U.S.A. prior to the nineteenth century when a Benedictine abbey was established in Pennsylvania in 1846. Between 1890 and 1960 most monastic bodies increased more than at any time since the seventeenth century.

6. Thomas M. Gannon, S. J., and George W. Traub, S. J., *The Desert and the City* (New York: The Macmillan Co., 1969), p. 159.

7. Dr. Carl Bangs, professor of historical theology, Saint Paul School of Theology, was helpful to me in providing suggestions and improvements for this brief historical background. Any shortcomings that remain, however, belong to me.

8. Charles A. Fracchia, *Living Together Alone* (New York: Harper & Row, 1979), p. 60.

9. Gannon and Traub, *The Desert and the City,* p. 50.

10. Donald G. Bloesch, *Centers of Christian Renewal* (Philadelphia: United Church Press, 1964), pp. 126-27.

11. Thomas Merton, from an essay, "Contemplation in a World of Action."

12. In Western spirituality meditation and contemplation are frequently used interchangeably. However, some writers think of meditation as more rational and investigative whereas contemplation is more intuitive and given to a greater sense of wonder.

13. Harvey Cox, *Turning East* (New York: Simon & Schuster, 1977), pp. 65, 66, 71.

14. James C. Fenhagen, *Mutual Ministry* (New York: The Seabury Press, 1977), p. 91.

15. *The Book of Worship for Church and Home* (Nashville: The Methodist Publishing House, 1964), pp. 382-88.

Chapter 5

1. Donald P. Smith, *Clergy in the Cross Fire.* (Philadelphia: The Westminster Press, 1973), p. 144.

2. The *Discipline's* section on ministry does not refer to ministry as professional, but as ordained. The term "professional" is used only in connection with theological degrees.

3. James D. Glasse, *Profession: Minister* (Nashville: Abingdon, 1968), p. 169.

4. Although we need care and support from ministerial colleagues, little strength has been derived from professional peers according to some studies. See Gerald J. Jud and Edgar Mills, Jr., and Genevieve Burch, *Ex-Pastors: Why Men Leave the Parish Ministry* (Philadelphia: Pilgrim Press, 1970), pp. 53, 94-95, and Smith, *Clergy in the Cross Fire,* pp. 126-28.

5. Urban T. Holmes, *The Future Shape of Ministry* (New York: The Seabury Press, 1971), p. 247.

6. *The Works of the Reverend John Wesley,* Volume X (London: Wesleyan-Methodist Book Room), "An Address to the Clergy," pp. 480-500.

7. Glasse, *Profession: Minister,* p. 169.

8. Carl E. Braaten, *Eschatology and Ethics* (Minneapolis: Augsburg Publishing House, 1974), pp. 147-48.

9. From a review by Don Browning of *Home from the War,* by Robert Jay Lifton, *The Christian Century,* February 6, 1974.

10. Yoshio Fukuyama, *The Ministry in Transition: A Case Study of Theological Education* (University Park: Pennsylvania State University Press, 1973), p. 117.

Chapter 6

1. Harvey Cox, *Turning East* (New York: Simon & Schuster, 1977), p. 109.

2. Charles A. Fracchia, *Living Together Alone* (New York: Harper & Row, 1979), p. 2.

3. Karl Barth, *The Word of God and the Word of Man* (Philadelphia: Pilgrim Press, 1928), pp. 43, 45.

4. American folk hymn, *The Methodist Hymnal,* 1964, p. 432.

5. Rev. John Wesley, *Forty-Four Sermons* (Sermons on Several Occasions) (London: Epworth Press, 1944), p. 139.

6. *Ibid.,* p. 150.

Chapter 7

1. Harvey Cox, *The Seduction of the Spirit* (New York: Simon & Schuster, 1973), pp. 115, 118.

2. James D. Smart, *The Rebirth of Ministry* (Philadelphia: The Westminster Press, 1960), pp. 94-95.

3. William K. McElvaney, *Good News Is Bad News Is Good News* (Maryknoll, N.Y.: Orbis Books, 1980). See chapter 7.

4. James C. Fenhagen, *Mutual Ministry* (New York: The Seabury Press, 1977), pp. 25-26.

Chapter 8

1. Peter Berger, *The Noise of Solemn Assemblies* (Garden City, N.Y.: Doubleday & Co., 1961).

2. Carl S. Dudley, *Making the Small Church Effective* (Nashville: Abingdon, 1978), pp. 70, 103.

3. Thomas Merton, *The Seven Storey Mountain* (New York: Harcourt Brace Jovanovich, 1948), p. 56.

4. One form of caring not suggested in Berger's categories is Christian care for institutions, both religious and secular—hospitals, homes, schools, and social agencies. I have not included this sphere of caring in the chapter's content although it is of immense impact in the life of the church and our society.

5. Milton Mayeroff, *On Caring* (New York: Harper & Row, 1971).

174

6. Victor Paul Furnish, *The Love Command in the New Testament* (Nashville: Abingdon, 1972), pp. 195-96.

7. From *The Christian Century*, "Why Are You Going to the Trappists?" an interview of Henri J. Nouwen, October 2, 1974, p. 908.

Chapter 9

1. In *Good News Is Bad News Is Good News* (Maryknoll, N.Y.: Orbis Books, 1980), I have written more extensively on the response of the church to various liberation theologies.

2. Walter Rauschenbusch, *A Theology of the Social Gospel* (Nashville: Abingdon, 1945), pp. 5-6. Rauschenbusch was professor of church history in Rochester Theological Seminary and had served as a pastor for eleven years in "Hell's Kitchen," the tough west end of New York City.